Contents

About the Series

ATD's What Works in Talent Development series addresses the most critical topics facing today's talent development practitioners. Each book in the series is written for trainers, by trainers, and offers a clear pathway to solving real issues. Interwoven with the latest findings in technology and best practices, this series is designed to enhance your current efforts on core subject matter, while offering a practical guide for you to follow. Authored by seasoned experts, each book is jam-packed with easy-to-apply content—including job aids, checklists, and other reference materials—to make the learning transfer process simple.

The What Works in Talent Development series is a unique core collection designed for talent development practitioners at every career level. To date, the books in the series include:

- *Starting a Talent Development Program*
- *Blended Learning*
- *Onboarding.*

Introduction

Have you just been asked to start a talent development effort in an organization? Perhaps the organization that employs you offered you an opportunity to start a new department. Or maybe you are a consultant who has had success with employee development in the past, and one of your clients has asked you to provide support for a larger effort. Or perhaps you've been hired as the first employee of a new department or direction for an organization that has never had an employee development initiative.

Whatever the situation, you've come to the right place to get started. If you are responsible for or helping to start an organizational talent development program, this is a good place to begin your journey. What can you expect? This book provides answers to many of your questions, but possibly more important, it poses additional questions that only you and your organization can answer. Answering them as you begin is crucial to ensure success.

Why Is Starting an Organizational Talent Development Program Important?

Today's organizations face challenges on multiple fronts. Many of you have heard of the VUCA (volatile, uncertain, complex, and ambiguous) environment in which organizations operate. Your organization faces many challenges related to the uncertainty of the future and the changes required to address it. The best organizations recognize that no single leader or employee can be an expert in everything. Organizations need all their employees to be the best that they can to:

- Stay ahead of the competition.
- Use global expansion as an advantage.
- Tap into advanced technology.
- Use data.
- Be competitive when attracting, retaining, and engaging talent.
- Ensure that employees are prepared to spark innovation.
- Create an agile, capable workforce that is responsive to change.

- Build a competent workforce and fill a leadership pipeline.
- Enhance individual and team performance and productivity across the organization.

Every organization faces its own challenges, but ensuring that the workforce is skilled and knowledgeable about how to approach those challenges is a critical step to reaching success. Developing talent and starting an organizational talent development program is the best way to stay a step ahead of the competition and the challenges of the VUCA world.

What Does the Organization Need?

A 2017 research report, *Rewriting the Rules for the Digital Age: 2017 Deloitte Global Human Capital Trends*, shows the big-picture reason an organization needs to have a coordinated talent development strategy and focus on employees. The research was extensive, including data from more than 10,000 business and HR leaders in 140 countries. More than half of the top 10 trends related directly to developing employees to create a high-performing workforce and talented leaders for a successful future. Here are the top six trends, with the percentage of respondents reporting "important" or "very important" (Schwartz et al. 2017):

- organization of the future (88 percent)
- careers and learning (83 percent)
- talent acquisition (81 percent)
- employee experience (79 percent)
- performance management (78 percent)
- leadership (78 percent).

Without going into any extensive detail, note that these six trends relate to learning in one form or another. Even the top trend addresses networks of teams that are knowledgeable and empowered to take action. Organizations are hoping to reorganize for speed, agility, and adaptability. Do your employees understand how to be agile and flexible when the need arises? Defining the organization of the future means that continuous learning is critical for business success—always on and always available.

How Can Learning Be Delivered?

The same Deloitte research shows that new methods are overtaking workplace learning. For example, video and mobile comprise the majority of Internet traffic, at about 55 and 60 percent, respectively. Mobile phones are used by more than 60 percent of the world's population, so it is natural to expect mobile to be a key learning delivery system (Hootsuite 2017). Thirty-five million people have enrolled in massive open online courses, or MOOCs, in the last four years, and 50 percent of learners use mobile for more than a third of their learning. Learning must be delivered faster. Software engineers report that they must redevelop skills every 12 to 18 months (Schwartz et al. 2017). Almost all professions echo a similar message.

When starting a talent development program, it's critical for you to think speed, agility, and mobility. Learning is constant across the entire organization, and the role of the learning professional is changing rapidly. We need to be prepared to lead these changes and focus not only on content, but also how to curate the content and bring people together for learning. We need to help our leaders understand what is required and help our supervisors understand their important role in developing their employees.

What Do Employees Want?

All employees want to learn and develop their skills. Development has become key to retaining employees. Because Millennials make up a large portion of the workplace, a number of studies focus on how development relates to retaining this group. For example, Gallup research found that 87 percent of Millennials value development in a job (Adkins and Rigioni 2016). Yet the majority also say they are not receiving as much development and learning opportunities as they would like (Gallup 2016). Millennials want development to be easily accessible and available constantly. Whether employees want development or not and how it is presented to them, it is clear that developing talent is crucial for organizational growth.

About This Book

The chapters in this book first define what a talent development program is and then explain why it's important, how to design one, how to implement one, how to determine the outcome, and finally what you can do to prepare for the next iteration and for the future. Each chapter ends with a list of thought-provoking questions, which serve to summarize the chapter's content and guide topics of discussion that you and your organization should consider as you begin your talent development planning. You will also find job aids, templates, and checklists to support your effort. A list of additional resources is provided so that you can continue to address your specific needs.

Chapter 1: Getting Started: What Is Talent Development? This chapter offers an overview of the many facets that can be incorporated into your program and urges you to sort through all your options. Considering what is possible in your organization is as critical as knowing how and where to start. Crucial to your first steps is involvement throughout your organization: How do you rate the organization's readiness? Who needs to know? Who needs to approve the effort? And who needs to support the effort? How do you prepare leadership? What role will supervisors play?

Equally critical is assessing the needs in your organization: What is lacking in your organization that a talent development program could address? What employee learning and performance gaps need filling? What policies, systems, structures, technology, and equipment are in place to support implementing a talent development program? The chapter offers ideas and recommendations that will help you answer these questions.

You may be thinking, "There are lots of questions that need answering," and you are right; however, none is more important than the decision about how you tie training to the corporate strategy. You can't wait until the end to determine success. You need to determine in advance what you will measure and how to evaluate it.

Chapter 2: Shaping the Future: Why Start a Talent Development Program? This chapter focuses on why starting a talent development program for your organization is critical, and presents reasons for you to consider starting your program sooner rather than later. It addresses the benefits to the organization and employees. Research and examples from several sources provide data to demonstrate the impact the effort can have on your organization's goals and employee engagement. This chapter discusses how an organization with a learning culture supports a talent development program, and suggests what you can do early to ensure a successful impact for your organization. Staying current with the changes in the industry is also addressed.

Chapter 3: Designing Your Talent Development Program: How Do You Start? This chapter explores how you begin designing a talent development program for your organization. There are many things to consider as you begin your design, such as your organization's rationale, what will be included, and identifying a business case. Tapping into what you learned in chapter 2, this chapter provides guidance for what needs to be in place prior to implementing a talent development effort. The most important lesson in this chapter is making sure your strategy matches your organization's strategy. You'll gain practical suggestions to ensure ease, clarity, good communication, budgeting, and other things important to your talent development program. The chapter is lengthy and comprehensive; however, that does not mean it incorporates everything that you need to consider for your organization. Pay attention to the needs assessment discussion and to the follow-up guidance about required mindsets.

Chapter 4: Implementing the Plan: How Do You Execute an Effective Talent Development Program? This chapter guides your implementation. You might consider this "how, part 2," because it is an extension of the pre-implementation "how" in chapter 3. You will consider what works best in your organization, what implementation decisions you will make, and how to incorporate the effort into your organization's current business practices. Of course, the meat of this chapter is the execution process. The chapter is long, but it still does not include everything you should consider.

Chapter 5: Transferring Learning and Evaluating Results: How Do You Demonstrate Success? This chapter takes you through a process to determine the level of success for implementing your talent development program. Can you demonstrate organizational success? Can you validate individual learner success? Can you determine whether the effort has improved employee engagement? Included are best practices and evaluation methods for the various ways employees learn and develop. The chapter also discusses the impact of talent development on learners and the organization.

Chapter 6: Planning Next Steps: Where Do You Go From Here? This chapter provides closure and includes topics that address the question, "Now what?" It includes recommendations for taking your organization to the next level and expanding your talent development program. The chapter also offers suggestions for how to stay ahead of the changes in the world, technology, your organization, and the talent development industry. Probably one of the greatest concerns is ensuring continued accountability for the effort—especially when the world continues to move faster and become more complex. How do you keep everyone in your organization focused on continuous learning?

How to Get the Most Out of This Book

This book sets you on the path to creating a talent development program for your organization. It is meant as a guide and overview for the topic, not an all-encompassing reference to deliver a detailed assessment, implementation, and evaluation plan. You'll gain enough information to get started, as well as a few tools and tips to point you in the right direction. However, to be successful you'll need to keep in mind the nuances of your organization and its needs. Because the book cannot cover every possible option, be sure to tap into the resources provided to take your exploration and deliberation to the next level.

Given the brevity of this book, paired with the comprehensive topic, we've had to assume your experience covers certain fundamentals:

- You have some background in the knowledge and jargon of talent development, such as instruction systems design, the ADDIE model, 70-20-10, andragogy, and adult learning principles, as well as some basic design elements, such as writing objectives and developing surveys.
- You understand strategy and talent development's role in organizational success.
- You understand the concept of learning organizations and practices that sustain a learning organization.
- You have some history of the profession and ATD, and know how the association supports talent development.
- You understand how we, as a profession, evolved from training to training and development to learning to workplace learning and performance to employee development and now to talent development, as well as the nuances of each.

Icons Used in This Book

Throughout this book, you'll find icons highlighting concepts and ideas introduced in the text.

Icon	What It Means
	Tips from professionals will make your job easier and give you ideas to help apply the techniques and approaches discussed.
	Tools identify templates, checklists, worksheets, models, outlines, examples, illustrations, and other prototypes that can be a useful place to start.
	Resources are the books, blogs, articles, or even people that you can access to add to the information you've gained already and take your learning deeper.

References

Adkins, A., and B. Rigoni. 2016. "Millennials Want Jobs to Be Development Opportunities." *Gallup Business Journal,* June 30. www.gallup.com/businessjournal/193274/millennials-jobs-development-opportunities.aspx.

Gallup. 2016. "How Millennials Want to Work and Live." Gallup News. http://news.gallup.com/reports/189830/millennials-work-live.aspx.

Hootsuite. 2017. "Digital in 2017 Global Overview." https://wearesocial.com/special-reports/digital-in-2017-global-overview.

Schwartz, J., L. Collins, H. Stockton, D. Wagner, B. Walsh. 2017. *Rewriting the Rules for the Digital Age: 2017 Deloitte Global Human Capital Trends.* Westlake, TX: Deloitte University Press.

1

Getting Started: What Is Talent Development?

In This Chapter

- An introduction to talent development
- Why starting with a clean slate can be good
- Ideas for how to build a learning culture
- The importance of tying talent development to the organizational strategy
- Four underpinnings that form a strong talent development foundation
- Initial considerations about measuring and evaluating a talent development program

All organizations have missions, and most probably have visions. To achieve both the vision and the mission, an organization requires people who have the requisite knowledge, skills, and attitudes (often shortened to KSAs) to meet its strategic and operational goals.

A talent development program creates the culture, organizes a system, and delivers the tools and processes to ensure that the organization is prepared to meet its goals. Development may occur because there are:

- business needs or requirements, such as increasing customer satisfaction or market share
- employee needs, such as learning new skills, upgrading current skills, improving or changing performance, or achieving certification
- changes in the environment, such as rewarding quality instead of quantity or teamwork instead of individual achievements
- future organizational needs, such as quickly adapting to change or seizing the next opportunity.

There are certainly other instances, but ultimately by incorporating the 10 areas of expertise in the ATD Competency Model, talent development increases employees' ability to accomplish their work competently.

What Is Talent Development?

If you ask three people to define *talent development*, you will get three different answers:

- The CEO will tell you it is the competency required to ensure the organization achieves its strategic and operational goals and provides a pipeline of leaders for the future.
- A manager will say it is the ability to accomplish the organization's work.
- An employee will say it is the way that employees meet the needs of their career goals.

So, who is right? They all are! Talent development is an effort supported and led by organizations to ensure that all employees have the right skills and knowledge at the time that the employee and the organization need them.

In the past (and even today in some organizations), when the topic of talent development, training, or learning arose in conversation, the immediate discussion focused on classes and catalogs. But the workplace has changed—immensely. That is not to say that formal training (for example, workshops, college courses, and instructor-led classes in virtual and traditional settings) is no longer valued. In fact, it plays a critical part of learning. The change occurring is that more emphasis is currently placed on the other ways employees learn—on the job and from others.

And this change requires a different view of learning. Employees expect to learn constantly, and because the workforce is more mobile and transient than in the past, if employers do not demonstrate that they value talent development, employees will leave to find one that does. Today more and more organizations see the value of talent development and its importance. The implication is that we, the leaders in learning—trainers, talent development professionals, employee developers—need to upgrade our skills and lead the change. We need to stay involved with and informed about the significance and meaning of talent development.

Talent Development Is Important to Organizations

As organizations continue changing rapidly, they need to develop employees at an even faster rate. However, because they can't always define the skills they will require, part of talent development is preparing for an uncertain future.

Developing talent is critical to ensure that organizations are productive and able to stay ahead of their competition. Thus, it's important for talent development professionals to encourage employees to participate in opportunities to further their learning.

Talent Development Is Important to Employees

Employees who are interested in career development take skill enhancement, training, coaching, and mentoring opportunities seriously. They understand that skill and knowledge improvements are essential to maintaining expertise that matches changing times, so they want to stay up-to-date on the most recent industry innovations.

The talent development function nurtures these employees to become reliable resources that benefit the organization. Acting as a joint effort between employees and the employer, talent development works to upgrade existing skills and knowledge in expectation of future requirements. Employees gain professional and personal skills that benefit them on the job and in other aspects of their lives. These efforts enhance employees' knowledge and increase their sense of contributing to something greater than themselves.

Start by Asking Questions

If you are just starting out with an organization or if this is its first foray into talent development, you should be asking lots of questions. To better understand what talent development encompasses—especially for the organization—begin with questions like these:

- How is talent development defined by the organization?
- How will talent development be tied to the organizational strategy?
- What are the key drivers?
- What are the organization's goals? What are the goals for employees?
- Is a culture in place that will support the learning strategy?
- What policies, systems, structures, technology, and equipment are in place to support implementing a talent development program?
- Why talent development? Why now?
- How are skills gained today?
- What leadership can you expect from the executive team? Will they champion the effort?
- What employee knowledge and skills gaps exist? What is expected in the future?
- How sophisticated is the organization's learning culture?
- What has occurred to date or what plans are in place to create a culture where learning is valued?
- Who are the learning champions at all levels of the organization?
- What will success look like?
- What tools will help measure success?

If you can answer even half of these questions, you are well on your way.

TOOLS

An "Organizational Readiness Checklist" is at the end of this chapter to help you identify the strengths of your organization and the pitfalls that may hinder success.

Knowing what your organization lacks that a talent development program can supply is critical. This requires discussion throughout the organization.

Get Started on the Right Foot: You Are Lucky

If you're reading this book because you are truly starting a talent development program, you are at a huge advantage. Sure! I know I'm not in your place right now, and I don't know how many loose ends you are trying to knot together. But I still contend that you are very lucky to be starting on the right foot. Why? Here are a few reasons.

Talent Development Emanates From the Organization's Strategy

You have the ability to tie talent development directly to the corporate strategy. A study by Brandon Hall Group (2016) shows that less than 8 percent of organizations with an L&D strategy call it very effective, and less than a third even call it effective. This does not mean that the training efforts themselves are not effective in delivering learning, or that employees are not acquiring new knowledge. What does it mean is that even if the execution is perfect, the strategy itself has little to no impact on the business. You have the opportunity to ensure that your talent development strategy is connected to the business and will deliver bottom-line results.

Supervisors Will Own Development

You can ensure that all supervisors and managers realize that effective employee development is "Job One" (to paraphrase a car manufacturer). In many organizations, employee development has been relegated to the human resources department or a training group. You have the opportunity to place that accountability squarely on the supervisors' shoulders. You won't have to break any bad habits of "it's HR's job" or "it's the learning department's job."

Employees Will Embrace Talent Development

You can establish learning as a continuous, on-the-job process, focusing on how employees learn from the work they do and the people they work with. Is classroom training the best way to learn for your organization? Perhaps not. You can create learning programs tailored to the way that employees need to gain access to content. In many organizations, talent development is less effective because it offers only instructor-led training programs, with little focus on what is learned on the job or from others.

You Will Be Viewed as a Leader of a High-Performing Learning Organization

As a strategic business adviser to the C-suite, you will gain respect as a brilliant designer for developing the best talent in the right place at the right time, because your strategy will match business needs. Talent development professionals are often seen as facilitators and may not have an opportunity to demonstrate their contribution to the organization.

If you are thinking that the talent development department is alone in this effort, nothing could be further from the truth. Talent development is owned by supervisors, managers, and leaders, so the success of your efforts will be determined by the degree to which you are able to hold supervisors accountable for developing their employees, ensure that leaders are champions of learning, and tie learning to corporate strategy.

The Most Important Rule: Tie Talent Development to the Organizational Strategy

Organizations continue to struggle with creating a talent development strategy that has a real impact on the business. Without a strategy, organizations lack the guidance necessary to design and deliver effective learning programs that boost both individual and organizational performance. Research shows that 14 percent of companies have no talent development strategy. But, the presence of a learning strategy is not the entire answer. If organizations that have a strategy do not believe it helps to achieve organizational goals, it translates into wasted time and money (Brandon Hall Group 2016).

According to that same survey, most companies recognized the importance of a talent development strategy and were focused on doing something about it. More than half said they were ready to begin aligning the learning strategy with the business strategy. Most significant is that high-performing organizations were even more prepared. Those organizations saw year-over-year improvement in revenue, employee engagement, customer satisfaction, turnover, and organizational productivity. High performers are in a better position to make these changes because they are far more likely to have an effective learning strategy already in place; 66 percent stated that their strategy was either effective or very effective in helping achieve business goals. High-performing organizations are 78 percent more likely to have an effective L&D strategy (Brandon Hall Group 2016). In a study conducted by ATD Research and Rothwell & Associates, 88 percent of respondents believed that aligning learning and business goals was a relevant challenge for organizational talent development needs today (Rothwell 2015).

Embrace the lessons learned in these studies. Make it a priority to align the talent development plan to the organizational strategy.

Foundations of a Successful Talent Development Program

Having key underpinnings in place before you begin designing your talent development program provides a foundation on which to build success. Here are four important considerations before you begin:

- Have a clear understanding of a learning culture.
- Appreciate how the 70-20-10 model can guide you.
- Understand that everyone is responsible for employee development.
- Be aware that employees need to take responsibility for their own learning.

Learning Organizations and Learning Culture

The concept of creating culture isn't new. Edgar Schein's *Organizational Culture and Leadership* introduced us to the importance of culture in 1985. Now in its fifth edition, it's considered one of the most influential management books ever published. According to Schein (2017), "The only thing of real importance that leaders do is to create and manage culture. If you do not manage culture, it manages you, and you may not even be aware of the extent to which this is happening."

The concept of trying to make an organization better through learning and generating a learning organization isn't new either. It's the reason why Jack Welch said, "If it isn't broken, break it," and Michael Hammer coined, "continuous intervention."

The Fifth Discipline

Peter Senge introduced many of us to the "learning organization" in *The Fifth Discipline* (1990), defining it as "an organization that is continually expanding its capacity to create its future." He further defines the five disciplines of a learning organization:

- systems thinking—concerned with the whole
- personal mastery—continually clarifying and developing proficiency
- mental models—assumptions, generalizations, or images that influence how we view the world
- building shared vision—a mutual picture of the future that fosters genuine commitment
- team learning—using dialogue to suspend assumptions and think together to ensure the organization learns.

RESOURCES

If you have never read *The Fifth Discipline*, do it now. If the last time you read it was when it came out in 1990, go back and read it again. I swear it takes on a new meaning today. Senge was ahead of his time in his thinking.

Although this book is not about building culture, a learning culture is one of the underpinnings of ensuring success as you design your organization's talent development program. Why? As Senge puts it, "Real learning gets to the heart of what it means to be human. Through learning we re-create ourselves. Through learning we become able to do something we never were able to do. Through learning we extend our capacity to create, to be part of the generative process of life." Those are powerful words. Learning is as fundamental to us as many of our other survival drives.

PRO TIP

Make sure your organization does not have a "learning disability." Senge wrote, "Learning disabilities are tragic in children, but they are fatal in organizations. Because of them, few corporations live even half as long as a person—most die before they reach the age of forty."

A Learning Culture's Impact

The research supporting ATD's whitepaper, *Building a Culture of Learning*, found that only 31 percent of organizations have a culture of learning. The research also found that top-performing organizations were five times more likely to have a learning culture, three times more likely to use the learning culture in recruiting, and three times more likely to hold leaders accountable for demonstrating learning's importance (ATD 2016). It is these statistics that embolden some organizations to use the term high-impact learning culture.

The learning culture concept encourages us to think about learning as an organizational process rather than an individual development process. This idea is critical given what we know about how we learn at work.

Building a Learning Culture

The Society for Human Resource Management defines a learning culture as "a community of employees instilled with a growth mindset" (Grossman 2015). At its base, a learning culture operates from a shared set of organizational values, assumptions, beliefs, processes, and practices that encourage individuals—and the organization as a whole—to increase knowledge, competence, and performance. You can diagnose your organizational culture and make changes to develop a learning culture; however, as you can imagine, there are many opinions about what is needed to build a learning culture. There is no "best" way or even a guaranteed way to build a learning organization. Nevertheless, there are some things to heed.

Most important, make time for learning and create accountability from the top down. This leads to the creation of individual development plans (IDPs). The ATD research report *Building a Culture of Learning* found that making IDPs part of a culture of learning requires:

- regularly updated IDPs for every employee
- employee accountability for the specific learning outlined in their IDPs
- nonfinancial rewards and recognition for employee learning.

Making time does not mean the amount of time invested in attending formal learning events. It means that organizations allow employees time on the job to learn, such as time to:

- Receive feedback from supervisors and then plan for how they can improve or change what they heard.
- Learn from a coach or a mentor.
- Learn by serving on a team, shadowing another employee, or creating a solution with an employee from another division or location.
- Discuss projects and updates with supervisors on a daily basis.
- Practice and reflect on what happened and what might be done differently in the future.

A true learning culture tolerates mistakes and celebrates creativity. It encourages risks and understands failure. Employees are allowed to try and learn and fail until they're successful. Finally, a learning culture has a process that employees can use to share what was learned for the team and organizational learning. A learning culture is a hallmark of a high-performing organization.

TOOLS

"Building a Learning Culture" is a tool you can use as a discussion starter with your senior leaders, or to initiate what is required for this foundational success requirement. You'll find it at the end of this chapter.

70-20-10 Guidance

If you say the word *learning*, almost everyone conjures up an image from school. This can sometimes lead to a restricted paradigm with a focus primarily on cognitive competency. It also brings to mind a delivery process with a teacher-student relationship, where learning must be transferred. In fact, most learning in the workplace does not occur that way.

Imagine you are at work and you need help. What do you do? Ask a co-worker for assistance? Check your organization's intranet? Review a previous task? Look in your employee handbook? Ask your boss? Google it? Sure. Any or all of these. You would not necessarily be looking for a teacher to help you. In fact, about 70 percent of what you learn is based on on-the-job assignments, and about 20 percent of what you learn comes from others in a social aspect. Only about 10 percent of what we learn occurs in the way you think of "learning." This must be taken into consideration when you start a talent development program.

Where do these numbers come from? In the 1980s, a team of research scientists from the Center for Creative Leadership in Greensboro, North Carolina, studied how successful leaders learn. They determined that 70 percent was learned as hands-on experience on the job, usually directed by a manager; 20 percent was learned through developmental interactions, now called *social learning;* and 10 percent was learned through formal learning, such as attending a class or reading (Lombardo and Eichinger 2011). Since the original work, the study has been replicated in many countries, by many organizations, and with many levels of employees with similar results. The percentages are not meant to be a formula, because they depend upon the organization and the individuals. Instead, they provide a guideline. So, what kinds of learning fit in each category?

Formal Content: 10 Percent

- courses, seminars, and workshops
- e-learning and virtual modules
- blended learning
- certification and certificates
- professional accreditation
- college or university classes
- MOOCs, CMOOCs, and SPOCs
- reading.

Learning From Others: 20 Percent

- being mentored or coached
- mentoring or reverse-mentoring and interviewing others
- online professional communities and blogs
- advice, opinions, and work debriefs
- curated or shared work
- internal or external networks
- 360-degree feedback processes
- research projects
- training or teaching others.

On-the-Job Assignment: 70 Percent

- problem solving, such as leading a project or action team
- cross-functional activities
- rotational assignments
- community or volunteer activities
- new responsibilities or acting roles
- stretch assignments
- change management activities
- new learning applications
- derail-proofing other employees.

As you design your talent development program, include a plan for how to encourage, support, and budget for all three kinds of learning.

Everyone Is Involved in Employee Development

Learning is not dependent on the talent development department. If you work for a small company and think that you are alone in your one-person talent development shop, think again. You are not. Talent development is everyone's business.

If you're used to HR owning organizational learning, prepare yourself for a new paradigm. Over the past few years, a huge role reversal has occurred: Leaders train and trainers lead (Figure 1-1). Organizations are now looking to trainers to lead organizational talent development effort and provide solutions. And although it has been a part of the role all along, supervisors and managers are now expected to develop their employees. Part of the talent development program should be to provide them with all the skills they need to do this.

Figure 1-1. The Great Role Reversal

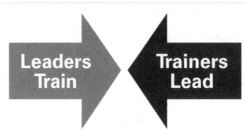

In her book *Communicate Like a Leader,* Dianna Booher (2017) says, "Make learning a topic of casual discussion and ask, 'What new learning opportunities have you been able to take advantage of since we last talked about your career?' Allow time in staff meetings occasionally (and with prior notice) for a few to mention a learning resource (blog, book, podcast, course) they have found helpful and would recommend to their coworkers."

You will want to improve your supervisors' and managers' coaching and development skills. What are the most beneficial skills your managers should have? Here are a few to get you started. Ensure that your managers and supervisors know how to:

- **Develop an employee's individual development plan.** This is a great place to start because it requires the manager and employee to have a discussion about career goals.
- **Offer development options beyond the job.** Well-rounded employees are a benefit to the organization. They learn new skills and obtain a better understanding of how the organization works if they have opportunities to develop in other departments or even in other organizations. Tools that managers have available include shadowing someone else, a stretch assignment, a rotational assignment, a job swap, or others.
- **Give feedback.** When feedback is delivered regularly and tied to examples employees learn incrementally. Feedback should be both constructive changes and reinforcing comments.
- **Set quantitative performance metrics.** Metrics tell employees what the goal is; incremental objectives are established so that employees see progress. Metrics should be discussed at least once a month.
- **Suggest networks.** Employees who link with others will grow from those relationships. Help them find mentors, coaches, professional associations, or a learning community of practice.

TOOLS

At the end of this chapter, you'll find the tool "IDPs: Who Is Responsible for What?" to use during an IDP discussion. And at the end of chapter 4, you will find "The 4 Cs," which provides guidance about how to facilitate a career discussion. Both will be helpful for your managers if they are new to the idea of developing their employees.

- **Invest.** Whether it is spending money so the employee can attend a conference, or allowing time to meet with an on-site book club, managers need to invest in their employees' futures.

- **Remove barriers.** If organizational processes challenge employee development, managers need to find a way to run interference. Make introductions, bridge departments, and find ways to help employees continue to learn.

- **Be a great role model.** Managers have an opportunity to model many things. One of the best things a manager can do is to demonstrate that learning is important. Managers also need to demonstrate how to accept feedback and be open to bad news. Finally, managers and supervisors need to invest in their own learning.

TOOLS

"ebb's Supervisor's Employee Development Ideas Checklist" is located at the end of chapter 4. Give a copy to your managers and supervisors so they have a handy list of ideas they can use to develop their employees.

There are many other things you can do to help supervisors and managers become better employee developers, including recommending books, offering a seminar, partnering them with other managers, providing coaching, or helping them find a mentor.

RESOURCES

The *Developing Employees (Pocket Mentor)* from Harvard Business School Press offers immediate support to managers who need ideas for how to develop employees. Its small size, handy tools, and practical advice will appeal to your managers who need to bolster these skills.

Individuals Are Accountable for Their Learning

The last consideration you should build into your foundation is that professionals are becoming more accountable for their own professional development. You may call it lifelong learning. Some use self-directed learning, but its definition is more prescriptive than the discussion here. It is often defined as "a training design in which trainees master packages of predetermined material, at their own pace, without the aid of an instructor" (Piskurich 1993). Self-directed learning has more of an academic implication than an adult learning one.

If employees are going to be held accountable for their learning, one would assume we all know how to learn. But, were you ever taught how to learn? It's not likely. Researchers from several universities found that the two ways we learn best is through distributed practice (practice over time) and practice testing (often used in MOOCs or even flashcards). Some tools we rely upon, such as rereading, designing a mnemonic, or highlighting what we read, are helpful, but less effective (Dunlosky et al. 2013).

RESOURCES

To find out more about learning to learn, watch one of these short videos:
- "Learning How to Learn," a TEDx Talk by Barbara Oakley (http://bit.ly/2vZo8LS)
- "After Watching This, Your Brain Will Not Be the Same," a TEDx Talk by Lara Boyd (http://bit.ly/29RKdNV)

Whatever you call it, learning is a strategic enabler whether you work for a corporation or for yourself. As employees have become more autonomous in determining the direction of their careers, they have become lifelong learners and continue to be strategic enablers (ATD 2015). This fact has an upside and a downside: The advantage is that the employees your talent development program serves will have a clear understanding that they need to take charge of their careers and identify which skills and knowledge they need and desire. The downside is that if your talent development program does not offer employees what they're expecting, they will leave and find employment elsewhere. Turnover is costly to your organization, so you need to stay informed about not only the development of employees, but what it takes to retain them.

Each of these four information blocks—learning culture, 70-20-10, managers as coaches, and individual expectations—fits together to form a solid foundation you need to build upon as you plan your talent development program. The rest of this book shows you how to start a talent development effort for your organization.

Jump-Start Your Efforts

What can you do immediately to begin creating your talent development program? Consider these fact-finding precursors.

Review Engagement Surveys

Engagement surveys include a great deal of information. Read your organization's last three engagement surveys, compare them, and look for trends. What do they tell you about the learning attitude? How can this information help you plan and design the talent development program?

Get Senior Leaders on Board

Executive support is essential for creating a learning organization and implementing a talent development program. Senior leaders manage the budget and identify business needs, such as increasing customer satisfaction, increasing market share, and improving quality. If you make sure the C-suite is on board, you can work with them to discuss their goals and then tie them to your development plans. Then you decide the best way to meet the goals and how you will know if you are successful.

Assess How Middle Management Approaches Development

Supervisors and managers will not have the same approach to employee development. Some will embrace their role as employee coaches, while others may not see it as part of their job description. Talk to them to find out where they stand. You could also look to retention numbers for more information—employees rarely stay where they are not developed.

Initiate Your Evaluation Plan

Although we won't discuss the evaluation plan until chapter 5, you need to begin thinking about how you will measure success. What tools are available to you? What do you anticipate your leaders will want to measure?

In *The Business Case for Learning*, Patti and Jack Phillips (2017) home in on the dilemmas facing the learning and talent development field:

- Learning and development is not used on the job as desired.
- Learning programs don't produce data to demonstrate how they make a difference.
- Talent development teams do not provide measurements desired by organizational executives.

Keep these challenges in mind as you plan how you will measure and evaluate your efforts. Consider how ready your organization is to not only implement a talent development effort, but also invest in the evaluation that will resolve these dilemmas: ensuring learning is transferred to the workplace, proving learning makes a difference, and delivering the data your executives desire. The ease with which you can do this will depend on the size of your organization, the talent development effort, your department, and your budget. It also depends on many of the other elements I've written about in this chapter and others, including involvement of your senior leaders, the attitude of your supervisors and managers, and you and your team's desires for success.

TOOLS

"Is Your Organization Ready for Real World Evaluation?" is an evaluation readiness assessment located at the end of this chapter. It provides initial considerations for your evaluation plan, which you will develop in chapter 5.

What's Next?

Whether you are a one-person department or the manager of several talent development departments; you work for a company of 100 or 10,000; or you are in a domestic location or multiple locations around the globe, you'll find many concepts and tools you can use to start creating a talent development program in this book.

It doesn't even matter if you are in a traditional talent development role. This book is for anyone who has an interest in starting and shaping a system that is larger than the traditional learning focus. You'll learn the whys, the hows, and the what's nexts of starting a talent development program. This book will show you "What Works" and will help your organization take a systems view of learning to become more flexible, agile, and innovative—and at the same time develop your employees.

When successful, the right talent development program helps great employees do an excellent job, and the return on investment goes directly to the bottom line.

Questions to Explore

- Why is talent development important to your organization?
- Why is talent development important to the employees of your organization?
- How do you intend to link the organizational strategy to your talent development program?
- How do you rate your organization's learning culture?
- How do you envision the 70-20-10 guidance fitting into the talent development program?
- What is in place to support formal learning? Learning from others? On-the-job learning?
- How do you think supervisors and managers will address their role as coaches to their employees?
- What role have IDPs played in your organization's culture?
- What reviews do you need to conduct to learn how policies, systems, structures, technology, and equipment will support a talent development program?
- How accountable do you think employees are for their development?
- What did the review of engagement surveys tell you about the organization's efforts for development?
- What are your initial thoughts about evaluation?

Tools for Support

Organizational Readiness Checklist

The Organizational Readiness Checklist will help you determine the degree to which your organization is ready to implement a talent development program.

You can use the tool in several ways: You can use it to determine areas of strength and weakness for your organization. You can also use it as the basis for a facilitated discussion with senior leaders. Ask each to complete the checklist and then review the scores with the group. Lead discussion around questions, such as:

- What are our strengths? Weaknesses?
- How can we use our strengths to shore up our weaknesses?
- What areas may hinder implementing our talent development program?
- How can you help to make improvements? How can I help?

Use the information you collect to improve their readiness level, as well as confirm buy-in of leaders.

Organizational Readiness to Implement a Talent Development Program	Not Even Close 1	A Good Start 2	Almost There 3	We Made It 4
A. LEARNING CULTURE				
To what extent do you believe:				
1. Learning is valued				
2. Individuals are given time to learn				
3. IDPs are expected of all employees				
4. Individuals are encouraged to manage their own learning				
5. Learning communities of practice are (or will be) encouraged				
Subtotal:				

Organizational Readiness to Implement a Talent Development Program	Not Even Close 1	A Good Start 2	Almost There 3	We Made It 4
B. ORGANIZATIONAL CAPACITY				
To what extent do you believe:				
1. Policies and procedures are in place, or an efficient way exists to initiate what is necessary				
2. The organization's mission reflects a commitment to employee development				
3. Human resources are adequate and available to introduce and sustain the talent development program				
4. Financial resources are adequate and available				
5. Resources are dedicated to supporting the administration of talent development				
Subtotal:				
C. INFRASTRUCTURE				
To what extent do you believe:				
1. Learning methods have been decided and are supported				
2. Authoring tools are in place for e-learning				
3. A platform is available for social learning				
4. Your organization has an LMS in place				
5. Employees have access to appropriate devices and equipment to fully participate				
Subtotal:				
D. ORGANIZATIONAL CLIMATE				
To what extent do you believe:				
1. Staff understand how the mission and goals of your organization relate to talent development				
2. Rewards and recognition are in place for learner initiative				
3. Employees know what they need to learn and why				
4. Open lines of communication are in place in your organization				
5. Innovation and creativity are rewarded				
Subtotal:				

Organizational Readiness to Implement a Talent Development Program	Not Even Close 1	A Good Start 2	Almost There 3	We Made It 4
E. SENIOR LEADERS				
To what extent do you believe:				
1. Senior leaders consider talent development a strategic necessity				
2. Senior leaders understand that talent development should be aligned with organizational, regional, or system goals				
3. Financial, mission, or safety reasons exist to implement a talent development program				
4. Senior leaders are convinced of the value of talent development and are committed to dedicating time to it				
5. Senior leaders are willing to work as a team and able to lead, model, and shape the talent development effort				
Subtotal:				
F. EMPLOYEE PERSPECTIVE				
To what extent do you believe:				
1. Continuous professional growth and development are desired by employees in your organization				
2. Employee preferences for learning were considered when designing the talent development program				
3. Employees are accountable for their own development				
4. There is a rationale for the selection of employees for learning opportunities				
5. Employees exhibit a collaborative, sharing attitude				
Subtotal:				

Organizational Readiness to Implement a Talent Development Program	Not Even Close 1	A Good Start 2	Almost There 3	We Made It 4
G. IMPLEMENTATION PLAN				
To what extent do you believe:				
1. There is an implementation team in place that represents multiple areas of the organization				
2. Talent development has been aligned with succession planning, HR, and other initiatives				
3. A plan and time exist during implementation to gather feedback from all who are involved				
4. There is a communications plan to share implementation progress with multiple stakeholders, regardless of their involvement				
5. There is a plan to monitor and evaluate the talent development program				
Subtotal:				
H. PRE-IMPLEMENTATION EXECUTION				
To what extent do you believe:				
1. Senior leaders have discussed and made an explicit link between the organization's strategy, mission, vision, values, and goals				
2. Internal marketing has been completed				
3. Managers clearly know their responsibility to develop employees				
4. Decisions have been made about the use of SMEs, external suppliers, and other experts				
5. Initial program components have been decided on				
Subtotal:				
TOTAL:				

Reprinted by permission from Biech (2017).

Building a Learning Culture

Use this tool to facilitate dialogue and learning with senior leaders throughout the organization, or as an initial road map for creating a learning culture. Strategies are loosely arranged in four categories, and each strategy leads to tactics.

Learning Climate

- ❑ Create and communicate a shared learning-organization vision.
- ❑ Align learning to organizational strategies.
- ❑ Ensure all employees have time to learn.
- ❑ Participate in mutual learning events with the community, academia, and associations.
- ❑ Encourage learning through teamwork.
- ❑ Accept and encourage risk, experimentation, creativity, and innovation.
- ❑ Celebrate learning and knowledge sharing through demonstrations.
- ❑ Focus power and decisions at the place of action.
- ❑ Ensure leaders value bad news.
- ❑ Encourage candor and dissent.

Learning Capability

- ❑ Create easy ways to store, curate, and retrieve knowledge.
- ❑ Operate from a systems thinking perspective.
- ❑ Create accountability from the top down.
- ❑ Ensure everyone has access to data and information they require.
- ❑ Embrace change and learn from failure.
- ❑ Celebrate informal learning.
- ❑ Provide multiple opportunities to learn.
- ❑ Acquire and apply relevant technology.
- ❑ Promote a growth mindset.

Learning Roles

- ❑ Foster collaboration, connection, and communication for learning.
- ❑ Expect managers to be mentors and coaches.
- ❑ Compel all leaders to be champions and models of continuous learning.
- ❑ Empower, encourage, and enable employees to learn.

❑ Include customers in the organization's learning.

❑ Expect continuous learning for everyone.

❑ Make learning a part of every job.

❑ Develop everyone as a leader, ensuring leadership is valued at all levels.

❑ Promote from within.

Learning Content

❑ Provide the skills to learn how to learn.

❑ Identify best practices.

❑ Develop creative and critical thinking skills.

❑ Learn personal agility, flexibility, and adaptation.

❑ Learn and practice dialogue.

❑ Seek and use knowledge wherever it resides.

❑ Recognize and reward learning that leads to action.

❑ Build capabilities for change.

❑ Teach how, not what.

❑ Link learning to performance.

Once you've determined which strategies will be best for your organization, you can develop tactics for each. For example, "foster collaboration, connection, and communication for learning" could be supported with these tactics:

❑ Create a climate of mutual respect so employees share with others.

❑ Design tasks that foster teamwork and shared responsibility.

❑ Encourage employees to join learning communities of practice.

❑ Establish a mentoring structure to help employees identify opportunities.

❑ Support peer groups that encourage discussion about career goals.

IDPs: Who Is Responsible for What?

Share this tool with managers who need a refresher on how to help employees with their IDPs.

Manager Responsibilities	Employee Responsibilities
The role of the manager is to initiate and be supportive of employee development, using company resources to do so. Managers: • Initiate the process. • Use company-provided frameworks for career planning. • Explain the IDP process and its purpose. • Provide an atmosphere of trust and open communication for their employees to discuss their careers and progress. • Guide the career and progress discussions. • Ask questions and listen. • Identify potential career opportunities for employees. • Identify learning resources and activities. • Provide constructive feedback.	While it's imperative for managers and organizations to facilitate employee development, employees have specific responsibilities. Employees: • Provide responses to career-related questions. • Self-reflect to identify career and development goals. • Evaluate skills and interests openly. • Draft an IDP with input from managers. • Be open to feedback and taking on new challenges. • Implement and own the plan. • Assess progress and initiate follow-ups.

Reprinted by permission from Hosmer (2015).

Is Your Organization Ready for Real World Evaluation?

Use this tool to identify your organization's readiness for evaluation. You may complete it yourself as preparation for your evaluation role. Or you may wish to have your senior leadership team (or your talent development team) complete the questions and use it as a discussion starter.

Is Your Organization Ready for Real World Evaluation?					
Check the most appropriate level of agreement for each statement (1 = strongly disagree; 5 = strongly agree)					
	Disagree 1	2	3	4	Agree 5
1. My organization is considered a large organization with a wide variety of programs.	☐	☐	☐	☐	☐
2. We have a large budget that attracts the interest of senior management.	☐	☐	☐	☐	☐
3. Our organization has a culture of measurement and is focused on establishing a variety of measures in all functions and departments.	☐	☐	☐	☐	☐
4. My organization is undergoing significant change.	☐	☐	☐	☐	☐
5. There is pressure from senior management to measure the results of our programs.	☐	☐	☐	☐	☐
6. My function currently has a very low investment in measurement and evaluation.	☐	☐	☐	☐	☐
7. My organization has experienced more than one program disaster in the past.	☐	☐	☐	☐	☐
8. My department has a new leader.	☐	☐	☐	☐	☐
9. My team would like to be the leaders in our field.	☐	☐	☐	☐	☐
10. The image of our department is less than satisfactory.	☐	☐	☐	☐	☐
11. My clients are demanding that our processes show bottom-line results.	☐	☐	☐	☐	☐
12. My function competes with other functions within our organization for resources.	☐	☐	☐	☐	☐
13. There is increased focus on linking our process to the strategic direction of the organization.	☐	☐	☐	☐	☐
14. My function is a key player in change initiatives currently taking place in the organization.	☐	☐	☐	☐	☐
15. Our overall budget is growing and we are required to prove the bottom-line value of our processes.	☐	☐	☐	☐	☐
Total					

Scoring

If you scored:

15-30: You are not yet a candidate for comprehensive measurement and evaluation.

31-45: You are not a strong candidate for comprehensive measurement and evaluation; however, it is time to start pursuing some type of evaluation process.

46-60: You are a candidate for building skills to implement comprehensive measurement and evaluation. At this point there is no real pressure to show impact and ROI, but this is the perfect opportunity to perfect the process within the organization.

61-75: You should already be implementing a comprehensive measurement and evaluation process, including ROI.

Reprinted by permission from Phillips and Phillips (2016).

References and Additional Resources

ATD (Association for Talent Development). 2015. *Managing the Learning Landscape.* Alexandria, VA: ATD Press.

———. ATD (Association for Talent Development). 2016. *Building a Culture of Learning: The Foundation of a Successful Organization.* Alexandria, VA: ATD Press.

Biech, E. 2017. "Organizational Readiness Checklist." Task Force Ocean Proceedings. Norfolk, VA: ebb press.

Booher, D. 2017. *Communicate Like a Leader: Connecting Strategically to Coach, Inspire, and Get Things Done.* Oakland, CA: Berrett-Kohler.

Brandon Hall Group. 2016. *State of Learning & Development 2016: Ready to Evolve.* Delray Beach, FL: Brandon Hall Group.

Dunlosky, J., K. Rawson, E. Marsh, M. Nathan, and D. Willingham. 2013. "Improving Students' Learning With Effective Learning Techniques: Promising Directions From Cognitive and Educational Psychology." *Psychological Science* 14(1): 4-58.

Grossman, R. 2015. "How to Create a Learning Culture." *HR Magazine,* May.

Harvard Business School Press, ed. 2009. *Developing Employees (Pocket Mentor).* Boston: Harvard Business School Press.

Hosmer, D. 2015. "The Manager's Guide to Employee Development." *TD at Work.* Alexandria, VA: ATD Press.

Kaiden, S. 2015. "Keeping Your Career on Track." *TD at Work.* Alexandria, VA: ATD Press.

Lombardo, M., and R. Eichinger. 2011. *The Leadership Machine: Architecture to Develop Leaders for Any Future.* Minneapolis: Lominger International: A Korn Ferry Company.

Marquardt, M. 2005. "16 Steps to Becoming a Learning Organization." *Infoline.* Alexandria, VA: ASTD Press.

Phillips, P.P., and J.J. Phillips. 2017. *The Business Case for Learning.* West Chester, PA: HRDQ Press; Alexandria, VA: ATD Press.

———. 2016. *Real World Training Evaluation: Navigating Common Constraints for Exceptional Results.* Alexandria, VA: ATD Press.

Piskurich, G. 1993. *Self-Directed Learning: A Practical Guide to Design, Development, and Implementation.* San Francisco: Jossey-Bass.

Rothwell, W. J., J. Arneson, and J. Naughton. 2013. *ASTD Competency Study: The Training & Development Profession Redefined.* Alexandria, VA: ASTD Press.

Rothwell, W., A. Zaballero, and A. Stopper. 2015. *Building a Talent Development Structure Without Borders.* Alexandria, VA: ATD Press.

Schein, E. 2017. *Organizational Culture and Leadership,* 5th edition. Hoboken, NJ: John Wiley and Sons.

Schwartz, J., L. Collins, H. Stockton, D. Wagner, B. Walsh. 2017. *Rewriting the Rules for the Digital Age: 2017 Deloitte Global Human Capital Trends.* Westlake, TX: Deloitte University Press.

Senge, P. 1990. *The Fifth Discipline: The Art and Practice of the Learning Organization.* New York: Doubleday.

2

Shaping the Future: Why Start a Talent Development Program?

In This Chapter

- The relationship between a learning culture and talent development
- How a talent development program affects an organization and employees
- Examples of the value of a talent development program and a learning culture
- Ideas to get a head start on implementing a talent development program

T alent development efforts are valuable to every organization. Continuous development brings benefits to employees and the organization. Employees are more successful with new responsibilities and have an increase in job satisfaction. Organizations may experience increased safety, reduced turnover, and increased productivity. Starting a talent development program takes a great deal of work, but the payoff is monumental. Talent development needs to be a priority.

The Rationale to Initiate a Talent Development Effort

We are living in times that are both stimulating and scary. It's still the same story: global expansion, lightning-fast technology changes, disruptive competition, unengaged employees, artificial intelligence. How can a talent development program create more excitement and less fear?

Certainly, you've heard it all many times. The world is changing rapidly, often described as being volatile, uncertain, complex, and ambiguous (VUCA). This has a huge impact on your organization, but you can help to manage that with a well-designed talent development program.

RESOURCES
If you want to learn more about the VUCA world, read *Leaders Make the Future: Ten New Leadership Skills for an Uncertain World* by Bob Johansen. Hint: If you have the hardcover version, remove the dust jacket and look at the inside.

Benefits to Your Organization

First and foremost, implementing a talent development program benefits your organization by:

- helping it reach its goals
- developing employees who are more productive and help to improve the bottom line
- increasing retention and reducing attrition
- enhancing learning agility to more swiftly respond to market demands
- heightening the ability to anticipate and respond effectively to change
- increasing innovation

- increasing customer satisfaction
- decreasing costs, rework, and time to market
- increasing market share
- keeping talent development aligned to organizational strategies.

Companies that invest in talent development experience numerous improvements, such as improved retention and communication (Joo 2010), and as unlikely as it may seem, investing in developing employees and working toward a learning culture can even enhance organizational innovation (Mallon 2010).

Benefits to Employees

Equally important is that implementing a talent development program benefits employees by:

- creating informed employees who are more aware of recent organizational changes and what is happening in the world
- enhancing employee knowledge and skills
- driving job satisfaction
- leading to a learning culture where all employees are motivated to acquire skills and knowledge
- improving the match between an employee and a job
- increasing morale, commitment, and engagement.

Notice that some benefits, such as improving the match of an employee and a job, may actually aid both the organization and employees. Great! Think of it as a double bonus. But can training really affect results? Ralph Alvarez, former president and chief operating officer for McDonald's Corporation, had this to say during an ATD interview:

> We made changes in training and saw quick impact. Our comparable sales are up; our guest counts are up; compliments are increasing; and our customer complaints are decreasing. These are all indications that the attention to training is paying enormous dividends. Our sales and guest counts are so highly dependent on training that we will slow down product releases if the proper training hasn't taken place . . . and we have data that show that the regions that have more people trained have higher sales and guest counts. (Bingham and Galagan 2007)

Helping employees shape the future direction of their careers is one of the most important managerial roles, yet this valuable task is often ignored or handled inconsistently or as an afterthought.

RESOURCES

The ATD research paper *Building a Culture of Learning: The Foundation of a Successful Organization* notes that top performers are five times more likely to have a learning culture and three times more likely to use the learning culture in recruiting.

You've likely heard reports that Millennials move from one job to another more often than other generations. A 2016 Gallup report, *How Millennials Want to Work and Live*, revealed that 21 percent of Millennials changed jobs within the past year—more than three times the number of non-Millennials who did the same. Gallup estimates that Millennial turnover costs the U.S. economy $30.5 billion annually. Why do they leave? The Gallup report makes two critical points:

- "Opportunities to learn and grow at work are highly important to Millennials when seeking out new jobs or deciding to stay in current ones."
- "Millennials don't want bosses—they want coaches. . . . Millennials care about having managers who can coach them, who value them as both people and employees, and who help them understand and build their strengths."

These are clearly related to ensuring the existence of a meaningful talent development program. Managers who take a personal interest in employees and their development build loyalty, and loyalty increases productivity. Talented employees want to be appreciated, advance, and gain skills to be more valuable to their organizations. Coaching, training, mentoring, and all their variations are paths to skill development. But it starts with the organization and its managers.

Why Advocate a Learning Culture?

Let's expand on the impact of learning cultures and explore why an organization would implement a talent development program. We can add to that by asking why an organization would also focus on becoming a learning culture—or moving on to the next level—why it would strive to have a high-impact learning culture?

Learning cultures and talent development fit together. A practical reason for advocating a learning culture is that it increases efficiency, productivity, and profit. It also seems to improve the employee mindset by helping employees develop a sense of ownership and accountability, which increases employee satisfaction and decreases turnover. Organizations with a learning culture are even more successful at implement-ing change and understanding how employees adapt to change.

> **A learning culture** is a community of employees instilled with a growth mindset oper-ating from a shared set of organizational values, assumptions, beliefs, processes, and practices that encourage individuals—and the organization as a whole—to increase knowledge, competence, and performance.
>
> **A high-impact learning** culture means that measurable results have occurred, which are attributed to the talent development efforts that support the learning culture.

Do data exist to support a strong learning culture? Studies by Bersin and associ-ates demonstrate that organizations with a strong learning foundation in place tend to significantly outperform their peers in several areas. Based on the research, there are many financial, operational, and employee-satisfaction reasons why aiming to have a high-impact learning culture may be valuable to your organization. By strengthening its learning culture, an organization can compete more effectively and boost employee engagement; for example, high-impact learning cultures:

- are 32 percent more likely to be the first to market
- have 37 percent greater employee productivity
- have a 34 percent better response to customer needs
- have a 26 percent greater ability to deliver quality products
- are 58 percent more likely to have skills to meet future demands
- are 17 percent more likely to be a market-share leader
- are seven times more likely to manage performance problems
- are 10 times more likely to identify and develop leaders
- are two times more likely to meet or exceed financial targets (Mallon 2010; Garr and Atamanik 2015).

A 2014 whitepaper published by Oracle describes seven steps you can take to implement a high-impact learning culture:

1. Integrate learning with talent management in support of capability development.
2. Encourage leaders and management to take ownership of the learning culture.
3. Make learning worthwhile and interesting. Prove its value.

4. Encourage employees to take personal responsibility for learning. Demonstrate the organization's commitment to development, starting during the onboarding process.

5. Embed learning to maximize experiential and reflective learning, as people work on real business problems.

6. Institutionalize collaboration, communication, and knowledge sharing by incorporating incentives and opportunities into every learning and performance process.

7. Drive development through redesigned and effective performance management systems, ensuring that performance is discussed on a regular basis throughout the year.

A high-impact learning culture would seem to be the ideal—difficult to achieve, but certainly worthy of the effort. A stellar talent development program can help organizations reach their strategic imperative.

Why Isn't Talent Development Always a Top Priority?

If developing employees is so important, why do organizations put off establishing a talent development program? If neglecting top-notch development efforts leads to turnover, why do organizations avoid revamping their old training departments and incorporating new developments? If limited employee development causes the loss of top talent, why do managers avoid their role to develop employees? Why is employee development a chronic problem, yet often ignored? Reasons often reside in three areas: lack of time, training perception, and lack of measurable return on investment. When these persist, talent development becomes an expense, instead of an investment.

Lack of Time

Probably the biggest reason talent development programs aren't created is that there isn't enough time. Organizations exist in turbulent times with competition coming from many directions. Even something as important as a dedicated talent development plan is often pushed to second place again and again. When *Harvard Business Review* asked Walmart CEO Doug McMillon about the pace of change, he explained, "Once upon a time, a company like ours might have made big strategic choices on an annual or quarterly cycle. Today strategy is daily. . . . As a CEO, you need to have a framework in your mind, but strategic thinking is much more fluid" (Ignatius 2017). We all tend to focus on the most recent, essential day-to-day requirement. If you've been asked to start a talent development program for your organization (or revamp a training department that no longer meets employees' needs), you are in a unique place.

Quiktrip Invests in Employees

Quiktrip is one of my favorite stores. It is a chain that has more than 900 stores in the Midwest and Southern United States. Every year since 2003, Quiktrip has been named one of Fortune's 100 Best Companies to Work For. All managers are promoted from within. Part-time employees receive 40 hours of training each year, and full-time employees receive two weeks of training in all aspects of the job. Customers are placed at the front of importance, and when the stores are busy, everyone stops what they are doing to assist customers. World-class manufacturing practices are applied, and every store logistics process is timed and standardized. Employees regularly discuss problems and offer solutions, their feedback is included in process redesign, and they are included as an important part of improvements made.

Based on this description, you probably would not have guessed that Quiktrip is a convenience store that sells reasonably priced, high-quality gas. It was one of the first two retailers to earn a Top Tier rating, exceeding the U.S. Environmental Protection Agency's standards for gasoline. While most organizations operate with fewer employees during slow times and cut employee development, Quiktrip does the opposite, maintaining fully staffed stores so that employees are available to fill in for others who are ill or take vacation. Its 13 percent turnover rate is less than a quarter of the 59 percent industry average. All this adds up to a good investment. Quiktrip sales per labor hour are 66 percent higher than the average convenience store chain. This is just one example of how an organization benefits by investing in its employees (Fortune 2015).

Training Perception

Perhaps an even greater factor is that the value of developing employees is still driven by past beliefs that employee development is grounded in a school-based approach. If you are starting a talent development program from scratch, you can create a corporate learning concept that has little to do with the traditional notion of education, schools, and teachers.

Lack of Measurable Return on Investment

Stop for a minute to take in the opening of this *Harvard Business Review* article:

> Corporations are victims of the great training robbery. Companies spend enormous amounts of money on employee training and education—$160 billion in the United States and close to $356 billion globally in 2015 alone—but are not getting a good return on their investment. For the most part, the learning doesn't lead to better organizational performance, because people soon revert to their old ways of doing things. (Beer et al. 2016)

Gosh! With an announcement like that, who wants to go any further? Fear not; there is a solution, and that's what we will be offering as an implementation plan.

From their research, Beer and his associates uncovered six managerial and organizational barriers that prevent employees from applying what they've learned—no matter how motivated they are:

- unclear direction on strategy and values
- senior executives who don't work as a team and haven't committed to change
- top-down or laissez-faire leader styles preventing honest conversation
- lack of coordination across functions
- inadequate leader time and attention given to talent issues
- employees' fear of informing leaders about obstacles to the organization's effectiveness.

Each barrier is based on the organizational design or lack of senior leader involvement. You will want to take each one into consideration as you start your talent development program.

TOOLS

Use the worksheet "What's in the Way of Your Learning Culture?" to explore barriers in your organization. It is located at the end of this chapter.

Financing a talent development program can be a challenge, and management's attitude toward your effort is crucial. Practitioners often get pushback when they want to try something new. This is especially true if the method requires a large layout of cash that does not seem to have a clear return on investment. Let's look at the story of Dare2Share, which should be encouraging to all of us.

Dare2Share was an innovative initiative conducted at British Telecom (BT) with the support of Accenture. The goals were to move to more informal learning, with networking and collaboration as the focus, and embed learning into the work employees do to close the gap between the two.

Employees were given flip cameras and taught how to create videos about tasks that they do on the job. They were then asked to post their videos onto a BT platform, which was similar to YouTube. No one was concerned about formality or much preparation or practice. The goal was simply to share what employees knew with one another.

Before the program was implemented, it typically took a department weeks to write a manual for how to address a new tool or process, and then employees were expected to find time to read the manual. Dare2Share eliminated the need for a manual (which was replaced with a couple short podcasts), shortened the design time (no manual to write), decreased the amount of time employees needed to learn the process, and presented an easier-to-understand method with actual visuals. Additional time was saved because no one had to deliver the same training message multiple times. Time saved is money saved, and BT made that work for them.

BT took the program one step further by allowing people to text or email the creator while watching the podcast if they had any questions or concerns. This led to more cross-functional collaboration and communication. BT certainly found a way to inculcate in the company the value of informal learning, collaboration and sharing, helping others, and how employees can contribute to the bottom line. Lack of proof of financial gain does not need to be a problem when planned well.

RESOURCES

You can watch a video about the Dare2Share social learning project at BT (http://bit.ly/2fciOL1)

You may also read a more detailed description of the case on the Towards Maturity website (http://bit.ly/2wUx8iK)

Get a Head Start

Are there things you can do before rolling out the talent development program that will positively influence success—sort of the "pre" roll out? Yes! Before you start designing and implementing your talent development program, instill the importance of lifelong learning, pinpoint the organizational values, and prepare for roadblocks and barriers.

Instill the Importance of Lifelong Learning

We've discussed creating a learning culture, but it takes three (some say seven) years to make changes in a culture permanent. Because a learning culture—or any culture— exists because of the shared values, assumptions, and beliefs of the employees, it makes sense that to change a culture, you will need to somehow change the beliefs of the people who make up that culture. A learning culture is to an organization as lifelong learning is to individuals. Even if implementing the talent development program is still a ways off, you can still begin to help individuals focus on their own lifelong learning. Help employees see that when they improve,

TOOLS

A "Career Development Discussion Guide" is located at the end of this chapter.

they grow, and foster the organization's growth too. Try these techniques:

- **Talk lifelong learning.** If this is a new concept, start talking about it. Write a blog post or feature someone in a newsletter who models lifelong learning. Tweet about it. Share articles that further your rationale.

- **Offer opportunities.** There are many ways to present learning opportunities. Get others to host a lunch and learn about their favorite topic, match employees to volunteer opportunities, start a business book club, or coordinate a self-directed learning cohort around a specific topic or work challenge.

- **Support managers.** Begin encouraging managers to focus on their most important job: developing their employees. Support them by sharing a career development discussion template.

TOOLS

Use "The 4Cs for Developing Others" tool to help your employees understand the specific tasks they like to do. You will find it at the end of chapter 4.

- **Make it a game.** What elements of games and fun can you initiate? Can you assign goals? Can you create challenges and prizes? How can you get senior leaders involved? It's not enough to communicate that lifelong learning is important. You need to embed it into the work employees do.

- **Establish an intermediary mentoring program.** Make it easy for everyone to have a mentor by creating an easy way for mentors and protégés to connect with one another. Provide some general guidance for the relationships—perhaps just a few rules and what mentoring looks like when done well. You may want to brush up on your mentoring skills by reading one of many great books available.

RESOURCES

An excellent book to get you started is *Mentoring Programs That Work* by Jenn Labin. Its tools and action steps provide a road map for how you can use the power of mentoring to initiate your talent development program.

- **Improve supervisors' coaching skills.** Make supervisors understand how important learning discussions and feedback are to employee growth and development. If supervisors know what skills employees want to improve and what goals they have, the supervisors will be more informed about future plans and how employees can contribute to organizational goals. If you coach supervisors who need to enhance their skills, you will be modeling how you want them to coach, while you are coaching—a metacoaching session!
- **Encourage learning events.** It is important that employees have time to learn on the job, but also encourage them to learn outside the organization. This includes professional conferences, association chapter meetings, virtual learning offerings, or even volunteer opportunities. Find ways to network within and outside the organization.

Pinpoint Organizational Values

You can also get a head start by determining what learning means to your organization so that you can customize your approach. What does your company value? This may include idea generation, technology, privileges, relationships, formality, what is rewarded, what is punished, having fun, leadership style, how problems are addressed, and others. Tailor your approach to the desired outcomes, based on the organizational values. If, for example, your organization values collaboration and teamwork, consider focusing on how employees can learn together. If you have independent, high-level individuals, consider a focus on self-organized learning.

Remember that one approach will not meet everyone's needs. Create opportunities that will appeal to all styles—not just what they learn, but also various ways they can learn.

Prepare for Roadblocks and Barriers

Finally, getting a head start means preparing for what could go wrong. No matter how much you think you've prepared the organization, you will still run into roadblocks. Perhaps a department is experiencing cuts to its budget; facing a decrease in market share for their products or services and possible extinction; or experiencing staggering growth and can't hire qualified employees fast enough. Layer over this the fact that you have employees from various generations who all like different learning modes. And virtual settings, which many organizations operate in today, often make instilling a learning culture even harder.

Mindsets governed by ego, fear, or complacency may be your greatest barriers. Edward Hess (2014), a professor at the University of Virginia, states that these mindsets can prevent employees from reaching their full potential. How is that possible?

- Ego is present because we all want to be perceived favorably and don't want to lose face or look uninformed. As a result, we deny or deflect new content. Defending ourselves prevents us from being open to new information.
- Fear prevents us from learning because we want to avoid the embarrassment of failure.
- Complacency occurs because we may take the easy way out, resisting new challenges and ideas (Hess 2014).

Recognizing these mindset barriers helps us understand our learners and plan how we can address them.

Other organizational aspects may hinder your plans to implement a learning culture. The best way I've found to identify and plan for potential roadblocks is to form a team, identify a list of possibilities, and brainstorm ways to address them, should they become an issue.

Early Efforts to Ensure a Successful Impact

The better prepared you are before you "go live," the stronger the impact your talent development program will have. It is important that you open the lines of communication with senior leaders and managers, as well as prepare your talent development staff for what is coming.

Communicate With Leaders and Managers

Begin communicating with managers early—especially if you are starting a talent development program from nothing. You'll need their support—both in time and budget—and the best way to achieve that is to involve them early, attain buy-in, and address any goals they have for the program. Be sure to tell them about the need for supervisors to develop their people and how the talent development program will support that.

Avoid waiting until you have all the answers. Find out what managers need and begin thinking about how you can translate their needs into your talent development efforts. What changes do they want to make, and how can those changes be measured? To ensure that leaders and managers help build a productive learning program, you need to begin the discussion about how you will evaluate the results. It is far easier to sustain a measured, successful effort than one that is successful but has no data to support the success.

Prepare Talent Development Professionals

Successful talent development programs are not based on last century's training model. You need to prepare your staff for the changes ahead. Share with them that everyone's role is changing and that they will begin providing more services than in the past. They will do as much coaching as training, and will need to be more focused on business needs, leading the development strategy, and shoring up their performance consulting skills. Staying current with today's trends and determining how those trends will affect the organizational strategy is crucial. They need to be fluent in 70-20-10, with an expanded role in the first 90 percent. In short, trainers are no longer order-takers, but development leaders in a consultative role.

RESOURCES
Consulting on the Inside by Beverly Scott and B. Kim Barnes is an excellent resource to share with any internal talent development professionals you have on staff.

Stay Current With Talent Development Trends

Identify talent development trends by first examining workplace trends. For example, a 2014 CEB survey of almost 34,000 employees at all levels reported nearly 40 percent of total work time was spent learning. Forty-one percent of today's U.S. workforce are contingent and not actual employees—but still require knowledge as if they are employees (Schwartz et al. 2017). Advances in artificial intelligence, robotics, and machine learning are creating a new age of automation as machines begin to match or outperform human performance, including cognitive performance. Some estimate that half of all current jobs could be automated by 2055 (Bughin, Manyika, and Woetzel 2017).

There is also a greater reliance on supervisors to develop their employees. However, even when this actually occurs, only 33 percent of employees agree or strongly agree that the available learning options meet their development needs (CEB 2014). Today's workers are overwhelmed, distracted, and impatient. They expect to learn on demand and collaboratively, requiring the flexibility to learn when and where they need it.

What does this suggest for the talent development profession? We need to focus on the 70 percent (on-the-job learning) and the 20 percent (learning that comes from others). We need to be prepared to offer learning that:

- is short, targeted, and relevant
- can be used in the continuous work and learn cycle
- can be acquired anywhere
- is available ondemand and continuously
- is curated
- can be used at the learner's pace
- learners can self-organize
- is useful in a collaborative setting
- is experiential in nature, no matter what the methodology
- increases employees' awareness of how to learn, not just what to learn.

Stay current by subscribing to professional journals, attending industry conferences, networking with other professionals, following blogs, and keeping your personal IDP up-to-date.

Ready to Move Forward?

Remember, your talent development program doesn't have to be elaborate. But it does have to be the best it can be for your employees and your organization. It has to be clear, and it has to have support—but it needs more than support. A talent development program needs to have the dedicated advocacy of the organization and its managers. When managers champion employee development and take the time to guide their employees to gain new skills and knowledge, the payoff will be substantial.

Chapter 3 provides a road map for how to start your talent development program—a plan for how to link development to the organization's strategic outcomes and begin thinking about the design.

Questions to Explore

- How well does your organization support a learning culture?
- What's the best approach to explain the benefits of talent development to anyone in your organization?
- What's the strongest argument for encouraging your organization to develop a high-impact learning culture?
- What are the biggest barriers to talent development in your organization? What can you do about it?
- What role do you see the talent development program taking in helping employees shape the future of their careers?
- Since employees are already overwhelmed, should you start to limit learning opportunities to those that are most relevant?
- How can you encourage employees to take ownership of their own learning?
- How can you get a head start in your organization's talent development efforts? What will ensure success?
- What does your organization expect of you?
- What's the most out-of-the-box idea you can think of that you would like to include in your talent development program?

Tools for Support

What's in the Way of Your Learning Culture?

Use this tool to consider why your organization may have a difficult time developing a learning culture. Encourage your team to determine what you can do to overcome current barriers.

Lack of Leadership Support

- ❏ Our leaders don't know the advantages of a learning culture
- ❏ Our leaders are passive or controlling
- ❏ Investment in learning isn't valued by managers
- ❏ The organization resists change and growth
- ❏ Leaders do not want to hear about mistakes or problems

Lack of Team Environment

- ❏ Personal accomplishment is rewarded over team accomplishment
- ❏ Individual expertise is valued more than teamwork
- ❏ Teamwork is viewed as a means to an end—not something to be valued
- ❏ We use a blame, not gain vocabulary
- ❏ We lack a knowledge-sharing method

Lack of Growth Motivation

- ❏ "That's not my job" deflects growth opportunities
- ❏ Mentors and coaches are not valued
- ❏ Learners are often prevented from transferring learning
- ❏ Employees are not given time to learn
- ❏ Engagement is low, and empowerment is rare

Short-Term Focus

- ❏ Putting out fires is valued over a future strategy
- ❏ We do not have a clear vision
- ❏ Problem employees are sent to HR for training
- ❏ Learning on the job is discouraged
- ❏ IDPs are not used

Opportunities to Improve:

Suggested Actions:

Career Development Discussion Guide

Share this tool with your organization's supervisors to help them talk with their employees. The discussions will help supervisors learn more about what each employee wants to do, what excites each of them, and what each employee wants to do in the future.

Current Goals

- What is your greatest strength?
- What do you like best about your job?
- What skill would you like to improve?
- How do you learn best?

Future Goals

- Where do you see yourself in three years? Ten years?
- What part of your job would you like to do less of in the future?
- What job or role most excites you?
- What is your ultimate career goal?

Support

- How can I help you in your current job?
- How can I help you achieve your career goals?
- What development do you think would help you achieve your goals?
- Who else can help you achieve your goals?

References and Additional Resources

ATD (Association for Talent Development). 2016. *Building a Culture of Learning: The Foundation of a Successful Organization.* Alexandria, VA: ATD Press.

Beer, M., M. Finnström, and D. Schrader. 2016. "Why Leadership Training Fails—and What to Do About It." *Harvard Business Review,* October.

Bingham, T., and P. Galagan. 2007. A *View From the Top: How CEOs Link Learning to Corporate Strategy.* (From the At C Level series.) Alexandria, VA: ASTD Press.

Bughin, J., J. Manyika, and J. Woetzel. 2017. "A Future That Works: Automation, Employment, and Productivity." Brussels: McKinsey Global Institute.

CEB Research. 2014. "Building a Productive Learning Culture." Arlington, VA: CEB Learning and Development.

Fortune. 2015. "100 Best Companies to Work For." *Fortune,* March, 149.

Gallup. 2016. "How Millennials Want to Work and Live." Washington, DC: Gallup.

Garr, S., and C. Atamanik. 2015. *High-Impact Talent Management: The New Talent Management Maturity Model.* Oakland, CA: Bersin by Deloitte.

Guerra-López, I., and K. Hicks. 2015. "Turning Trainers Into Strategic Business Partners." *TD at Work.* Alexandria, VA: ATD Press.

Hess, E. 2014. *Learn or Die: Using Science to Build a Leading-Edge Learning Organization.* New York: Columbia Business School Publishing.

Hosmer, D. 2015. "The Manager's Guide to Employee Development." *TD at Work.* Alexandria, VA: ATD Press.

Ignatius, A. 2017. "We Need People to Lean Into the Future." *Harvard Business Review,* March-April.

Joo, B.K. 2010. "Organizational Commitment for Knowledge Workers: The Roles of Perceived Organizational Learning Culture, Leader-Member Exchange Quality, and Turnover Intention." *Human Resource Development Quarterly* 21(1): 69-85.

Labin, J. 2017. *Mentoring Programs That Work.* Alexandria, VA: ATD Press.

Mallon, D. 2010. *High-Impact Learning Culture: The 40 Best Practices for Creating an Empowered Enterprise.* Oakland, CA: Bersin & Associates.

Oracle. 2014. "Seven Steps to Building a High-Impact Learning Culture." Oracle: Human Capital Management. www.oracle.com/us/chro-docs/june-2013-chro-deck4-1961622.pdf.

Schwartz, J., L. Collins, H. Stockton, D. Wagner, B. Walsh. 2017. *Rewriting the Rules for the Digital Age: 2017 Deloitte Global Human Capital Trends.* Westlake, TX: Deloitte University Press.

Scott, B., and B.K. Barnes. 2011. *Consulting on the Inside: A Practical Guide for Internal Consultants.* Alexandria, VA: ASTD Press.

3

Designing Your Talent Development Program: How Do You Start?

In This Chapter

- Presenting a process to design a talent development program
- Implementing the business elements of the program
- Creating a talent development program strategy
- Selecting topics and content
- Meeting the expectations of today's learner

Okay, so you are sold on the idea of a talent development program. You know what it entails, and you know why it's important. The next step is figuring out how to get started. This chapter will show you how to begin developing a strategy to design your talent development program.

When you initiate the design of a talent development program, you'll want to be sure you're spending your money wisely. Creating an overall strategy to steer your plans for employee development and ensuring that your talent development strategy links into your organization's strategy is the best way to start. This ensures that your plans address efficiency, effectiveness, and are economically smart. Let's look at a process for how to do that.

The Pre-Implementation Stage

Whether you were hired by an organization to establish a new talent development program or the task was delegated to you by your current organization, you have a great deal of work ahead. This section will define the steps you need to take to get started.

Or perhaps you were asked to upgrade or improve a talent development program that is already operating in your organization. Does the current program generate the results that the organization had hoped it would? Often the reason a talent development program is not living up to expectations is that the organization was in a hurry to begin and did not work through all the necessary steps. If this is the case, the process outlined in this book may hold the key—try taking a couple steps back and complete any research that was missed or ignored.

You may simply be trying to build a case to implement a talent development program for your organization. You see the benefits and want to sell that vision—perhaps your organization faces many challenges, and you know that it would benefit from a strategically developed workforce and a culture of learning. Chapters 1 and 2 provide you with data and data sources about superior performance in other organizations that is attributed to learning cultures. This chapter will let you in on what's ahead if your organization agrees to your plan.

No matter the situation, your task is to create a strategy supporting the organization and employees that executive leaders can embrace and buy into. You need to establish goals and objectives that not only support the strategy, but also can be used as part of the evaluation process to determine how the investment in talent development reinforces the organizational goals.

There are many situations that led you to where you are and why you are reading this book. Whatever they are, your initial step is to write a strategic plan for the talent development program. By showing how the talent development program will contribute to organizational success, you can change the view of employee development from an expense to contributing to the bottom line. Before you write the strategic plan, you will want to complete some background research. Let's take a look at how you might do that.

Conduct Research for the Talent Development Strategic Plan

Researching for the talent development program's strategic plan begins by building a rationale. Why are you starting a talent development program now? While you can include many different things in your research plan, I find that three options are particularly helpful: building a business case, completing a SWOT analysis, and interviewing employees and leaders.

Build a Business Case

Think of this step as making your case for a talent development program. You may be thinking, "But the senior leadership team has requested a talent development program. Why should I 'make a case' for it?" There are many reasons:

- Although your senior leadership team agreed, some may not have "agreed" as enthusiastically as others. Making the case requires you to gather data, define a rationale, and deliver supporting arguments.
- The members of today's senior leadership team may not all be there in six months when you are ready to roll out the program. Having a well-designed plan will be an advantage as you educate the new arrivals.
- Even if the senior leadership team is supportive, the program will also require the next levels of management and employees to also approve. Building a business case prepares you for those discussions.
- Finally, do it for you! A well-thought-out case puts you in the driver's seat when you are quizzed by others about why the organization is investing in talent and development.

PRO TIP

When senior leaders know that your focus is consistent and supports the organization's goals, they are more likely to partner with you.

So, where do you start to build a case? Following these five steps will inform, prepare, and enlighten you at this stage.

1. Begin by examining your organization's strategy. Training, learning, development, talent, and HR departments are seldom viewed as strategic because they are often putting out daily fires. This is a chance to start strategically—review your strategic plan, learn more about the organization's customers and competitors, and determine how your organization is viewed from the inside and the outside.

TOOLS

A tool at the end of this chapter, "Explore Your Organization's Strategic Priorities," can get you started on this task.

2. Identify how talent development can contribute to organizational priorities. Does the organization have new priorities? Is it having difficulty with current priorities? What skills, knowledge, and attitudes do employees require to ensure efficient attainment? You may need to expand your thinking to several layers, so get others involved. For example, several years ago, my company helped a client move into the European market. We knew that employees would need certain traits to succeed, including cultural sensitivity, flexibility, emotional stability, and openness to adventure. They also needed to learn about the traditions and customs of the area. The learning department started the research and created learning events for employees who were moving abroad, as well as those remaining in the Minneapolis area who would interact with the company's new European employees.

PRO TIP

A mind map works well to identify what knowledge, skills, and attitudes are necessary to address the strategic priorities. Place each priority in the center of the map and then identify what employees will need. Take your mind maps to the departments that are primarily and secondarily related to each priority for additional input.

3. Determine the metrics you might be able to use. To demonstrate the effect on the organization's top and bottom lines, you will need to measure outcomes. No single set of metrics will apply every time, so talent development professionals need to consider a variety of possibilities. Some metrics are easy to measure, such as increasing retention, while others are more difficult, such as ensuring employees are agile learners. The difficult ones require you to dig down into the layers of results. Research other organizations to gather valid data you can use to predict improvements for your organization.

4. Create a big-picture budget to balance the success metrics. Design it as a case study, so no one will expect exact numbers. Again, tap into your network to research other organizations. Obtaining data and examples from them will be valuable.

5. Create a pitch your CFO will buy. The key for every organization, for-profit and not-for-profit alike, is return on investment. This means that your mindset needs to focus on how you will create organizational value. Your CEO should see the talent development program as an investment—not a cost. If you can make a strong business case and have measures in place to show how talent development could contribute to the bottom line, you'll have a much better chance of getting support from your senior leaders. Building a case means you need to do your homework. A case that clearly shows how your talent development program offers a return on investment is a great place to start.

Complete a SWOT Analysis

SWOT is an acronym for *strengths, weaknesses, opportunities,* and *threats.* These are traditional bases of information used in strategic planning. Just as you would complete a SWOT analysis during an organization's strategic planning session, it is also important when you are gathering data to determine a talent development strategy. Invite stakeholders, including managers of key departments, to help you complete the SWOT analysis. You must be very deliberate in figuring out what can go wrong as well as what can go right. This tool can help you identify any unintended consequences of your plan.

TOOLS

A tool at the end of this chapter, "SWOT Analysis," is designed to help you prepare to develop your talent development strategy.

Interview Employees and Leaders

Although time-consuming, this step is my favorite. Schedule interviews with as many leaders and employees as you can. I am always pressed for a number here, so let me say that 30 or 40 is not too many. Whom do you interview? Start with senior-level leaders because they will help give you direction. Think about interviewing a diagonal sampling throughout the organization to get people from all departments and at all levels. At the very least, you should interview informal leaders, idea people, and negative people. Negative? Really? Yes. They will help you identify barriers you could face in the future. Use this information to begin preparing for potential barriers, and maybe even how you could prevent them from occurring.

Define the core questions you want to ask during your interview. Although you'll customize the individual interviews, these questions will help you uncover information to include in your talent development strategic plan:

- What is your vision for the talent development program?
- What do you hope we accomplish the first year? The second year?
- What do you hope we accomplish within five years?
- What should the talent development department be responsible for?
- What are the strategic priorities we should focus on? Can you prioritize them?
- What knowledge, skills, and attitudes do our employees need to accomplish strategic priorities?
- Who should have access to talent development services?
- What kind of services should talent development offer?

Plan to spend 45 minutes in each interview and try to schedule 15 minutes between each. End each interview with a question like, "Is there anything I missed or anything you want to tell me that we haven't discussed?" Meet on their turf and at their convenience, and always follow up with a thank you note. I recommend a handwritten note, although email or texts may be appropriate in your organization. Thank your interviewees for taking time out of their busy schedules to enlighten you about their needs and the organization's requirements.

TOOLS

A tool at the end of this chapter, "Interview Questions to Ask," offers additional suggestions on how to start this task.

Write the Talent Development Program Strategic Plan

Once you have completed your research, you are ready to begin to develop your strategic plan. You will find that the research you used to build a case study will slip right into your strategic plan. You probably aren't surprised to learn that a talent development strategy includes some of the same components as an organizational strategy: vision, mission, and learning philosophy or principles. You will also need to add how they align with the direction of your organization.

Vision

Your vision will define your lofty goal—your ideal endpoint. It should resonate with all members of the organization and help them feel pride and excitement about the possibilities. A vision should be something that is possible, but perhaps a real stretch to achieve. Think about your organization and how that stretch vision will help it achieve its strategic imperative.

Mission

Think about all the things you plan to do. A mission statement is like an executive summary of that. Will the talent development program be responsible for employee assessment? For engagement surveys? For college credit education? For supporting IDPs? Coaching? Establishing a mentoring program? For leadership development or a host of other things? What is the relationship between HR and the talent development program? Spell it out.

Philosophy or Principles

It's your choice whether you write guiding principles or a learning philosophy. However, you should consider at least one to ensure that your organization understands what the talent development program stands for.

Learning and development consultant Brent Schlenker believes that learning principles are "good to have when you need to make sure your team and stakeholders are grounded on your basic ideals before moving on to strategy conversations." This is the very reason I suggest that you think through the purpose and philosophy of talent development in your organization. When Brent delivered a session at the ATD 2015 International Conference & Exposition, he presented five guiding principles for training departments, which are highlighted in the sidebar.

Guiding Principles for Training Departments

We are knowledge brokers.
We build expertise in those who need it by leveraging those who have it.

We put people first and technology second.
We recognize the best training is often 1:1, but that doesn't scale. We strategically use technology to amplify, and efficiently scale up, the human element of training.

We build as we deploy.
We iteratively develop scalable solutions while meeting current and immediate training needs.

We see learning as a long-term process.
We believe training events are only a part of the journey toward expertise. We leverage multiple content delivery channels to make content more readily available on demand in real time.

We measure to evaluate success.
We ensure the effectiveness of training solutions by linking desired outcomes to business performance indicators, and tracking and evaluating results.

Adapted from Schlenker (2015).

Your mission, vision, and philosophy must align with the organizational culture they support. It will also be critical that senior leadership agrees to ensure consistency of purpose. If you are not creating from the ground up and you already have a mission and vision, be sure to compare all your documents. Are they consistent, and do they specifically state what you believe, why you exist, and how you will implement the talent development program?

PRO TIP

"Your training strategy must be consistent with the culture of the organization."
—John Coné, *ASTD Handbook, 2nd Edition*

Whom and How You Serve

This section of the talent development program strategy should clearly identify the employees you will serve. You may, for example, have primary clients and secondary clients. Does your organization have multiple divisions? Locations? Is there a hierarchy of service, or is it dependent upon who schedules your time first? If you are creating a new talent development program, you will need to depend upon the organizational culture, design, and infrastructure, as well as your own common sense. How you deliver value to your customers should also be addressed—you will base this on what your customers want and how they want it.

Your business model will cover the who and the how. You may include some of these elements:

- Your value proposition—What is the value you offer your clients? Why you?
- Customers—Who is your target audience? How do you know what they need?
- Product portfolio—What will you offer (classes, webcasts, coaching)?
- Services—Will you provide informal learning design, enrollment in college courses, mentor and protégé matching, or team building?
- Distribution plan—How will you deliver products and services? How will you communicate their availability?
- Organizational structure—How many employees will you need? What certification, degrees, and expertise will they have? What will they do?
- Financial model—Where will the money come from, and what will it be used for? Will it be centrally funded, will departments have their own budgets, or both? (This is a big-picture overview for the strategy; we'll address budgeting later in this chapter.)

Strategic Direction

The strategic direction gives you the opportunity to look toward the future. Where are you now, and where are you planning to take the talent development program? What goals do you have near term and for the future? Consider your strategic and program goals, as well as your key strategies and initiatives. This is a great time to review what you learned when you were developing the business case.

Anyone who reads a strategic plan expects to see this section. It is also a good place to state how you intend to stay in touch with the organization's strategic priorities. How do the initiatives and strategies support the organization's priorities and solve its issues? Are your initiatives acceptable to the organization? Your strategies could include:

- developing employee competencies
- onboarding development
- implementing new content
- initiating new delivery systems
- adding new services
- increasing the number of customers.

Include your plan for how the talent development program will reach its strategy. This is where you list the requirements you have for things such as data, space, technology, equipment, leadership support, and, of course, financial support.

Evaluation

End your strategy by identifying the indicators of success. How will you measure success? How will you demonstrate efficiency, effectiveness, and quality, as well as how the design meets the needs of the organization? Present a high-level evaluation plan: what and how you expect to evaluate the results. You'll add more details once the strategy has been approved. (Chapter 5 covers this in more detail.)

Executive Summary

Once you've written the strategy, develop an executive summary. Even though it is placed at the beginning of the document, it's easier to summarize what you've written after you've written it.

Distribute the Strategy

Identify all the individuals who need to read and approve your strategic plan. Certainly, you need to start with approval from your direct manager. The leadership team should comment on the plan and advise you of any potential risks and changes that may be beneficial. As soon as you have the support of all the individuals who need to sign off, use this as an initial communication plan throughout the organization. This strategy is a tool that allows you to be proactive in your approach to starting your organization's talent development program. It leads to buy in, prepares you to make better decisions, and ensures that you will get better results.

Taking Care of Business

Your strategy has been approved and you're ready to start. But where? What do you do first? Remember, the most important role the talent development program plays is to support the organization in reaching its strategic priorities. Your organization expects a return on its investment in training, and aligning the training to organizational requirements is the underlying reason why you are on the payroll. The better you tie the training delivered to your organization's goals, the more successful your talent development program will be.

Setting up a talent development program requires you to be organized and efficient. Make sure you review the purpose, establish governance, develop a budget, and consider all you need to do to manage the talent development program.

Align Employee Development to Organizational Goals

When designing, buying, or delivering a training program, you need to start with the business goal to ensure that employee development is aligned to organizational requirements. Goals typically fall into a few general categories:

- **Expense reduction.** Refresher courses or job aids might be required to decrease errors or rework a procedure; new information might be used to reduce reliance on more expensive support from consultants or other organizations; new information might also be aimed at increasing employee productivity.
- **Revenue generation.** Sales training is usually aimed at increasing sales; customer-satisfaction development may be aimed at ensuring that customers return or recommend products or services to others. This category could also be aimed toward innovation and developing new products or services.
- **Regulation compliance.** The government or industry might require organizations to provide a webcast to prevent errors or fines from regulatory agencies.

Figure 3-1 presents a visual of how to link your business strategy to learners' development of knowledge, skills, and attitudes.

Figure 3-1. Linking Learner Development to Business Goals

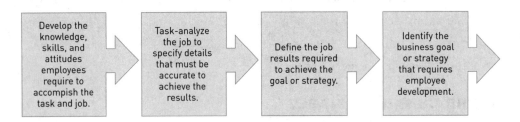

Always know how the learning approach you have planned addresses organizational requirements. What does your organization need? And at times, you'll need to know what employee development your organization does not need. How can that be?

Sometimes, management asks for training even though training is not the solution. For example, if one of your organization's goals is to increase customer satisfaction, no amount of training is going to achieve the goal if the real problem is a slow delivery of product from distribution. Even if training is part of the solution, it is rarely the entire solution. A systems approach is usually required to accomplish most goals—that is, examining the entire set of inputs (materials, people, equipment, processes, and environment) and aligning them with the goal.

You will have challenges along the way, but none as critical as keeping your talent development program focused on what benefits the organization the most. Organizations achieve alignment when learning is a business asset and permeates the culture. Talent development must go beyond the delivery of courses, programs, and modules to ensure learning becomes part of the business. Even fully committed organizations find it tricky to maintain that alignment, and challenging to measure whether it exists. One study found that the most common alignment barrier is the learning organization's lack of a complete understanding about the business (ASTD and i4cp 2012). So, even though I've been preaching alignment, you also have to understand the business to which you are aligning.

TOOLS

A checklist, "Align Employee Development to Organizational Strategy," at the end of this chapter will help keep you on the straight and narrow during this stage and at the execution stage.

Establishing Talent Development Governance

Governance is the formation of policies and standards to provide guidance for the talent development program. You'll also consider how to monitor them, ensuring that the organization's plans are implemented the way they were originally intended.

Policy

Use your mission statement and other elements in your strategic plan to ensure your content is consistent. The simplest policy includes:

- A value statement that proclaims what the talent development department values (as opposed to the value proposition in the strategic plan—the value you offer customers). For example, a talent development department could value innovation, speed, and quality.
- A belief statement that clarifies your beliefs in how talent development affects employees and the organization. It could state, "We believe that all employees need to be actively involved in their own development" or "The organization is committed to providing development for all employees to ensure they are contributing members of the organization and society."
- An action statement that defines what talent development will do.

TOOLS

A "Policy Development Template" is located at the end of this chapter. Use it to begin your writing.

Why do you need a policy? It helps everyone who is delivering talent development services coalesce as a team and focus on what is most important to the organization. It can also assist with establishing priorities around budget, schedules, and decisions about content.

What is included in the policy? You can't include everything, but you might consider some of these areas if they pose a concern: safety, developing new skills, diversity and inclusion, customer service, organizational strategy, leadership, productivity, and communications. You may also want to include elements of how you plan to design and deliver products and services, such as:

- evaluation of talent development efforts and programs
- selection of employees who attend special events
- whether development opportunities will be mandatory or voluntary
- location and timing of learning events
- programs to be established and added to the portfolio
- design and delivery standards
- tuition-paid plans
- external services and programs
- how priorities will be established
- linking talent development to performance reviews
- stating how often the policy will be reviewed and updated.

How do you develop the policy? It is not something you should sit in front of your computer at the last minute and pound out. The true value of a talent development policy occurs when many people are involved. If you have staff, perhaps you could start by brainstorming a list of things to include in the policy. If you are working alone, write a draft and meet with several leaders or informal leaders whose opinions you respect for input. The discussion is where the most value occurs.

PRO TIP

The best talent development policy is created after multiple iterations. Develop your policy and keep notes about the challenges you face for the first six months. After six months, review the policy with a team of stakeholders and make changes, additions, or deletions.

Once the policy is completed, how can you use it? Share it with new employees to explain the organization's beliefs about learning. Give copies to all supervisors to include in their employee performance discussions. Include it in packets, physically or electronically, during talent development events. Explain changes and updates to senior leaders and managers. Blog about it to show what is in the policy, how it is implemented, and how it relates to the organization's strategic initiatives.

The talent development policy is important for clarifying what you believe in. It helps focus and motivate employees responsible for developing others, while giving everyone something to visualize and an incentive to set higher goals.

TOOLS

To help you develop your policy, refer to the tool at the end of this chapter, "An Example of a Simplified Talent Development Policy."

Standards

Talent development requires guidelines, or standards, to define the measures of success. Successful organizations understand what skills they expect employees to demonstrate, and these skills are often tied to development events. But there are other metrics that may be important. The measures or indicators a talent development professional uses should represent factors that lead to the organization's strategic imperative: improved customer, operational, financial, and societal performance. Bruno Neal (2014) suggests that common quality indicators of success may include:

- how departments set achievement standards and attain them
- the amount of time dedicated to instructional issues during staff meetings (less is better)
- the quality of instruction as rated by learners
- the expenditure for development per employee.

Several methods can be used to identify and measure the quality of a service or product, including ISO guidelines, Baldrige principles, or curriculum review. Standards offer a way for talent development professionals to compare their program with other organizations.

RESOURCES

The February 2014 *Infoline*, "How to Develop Training Quality Standards," by Bruno Neal, describes several methods that can be used to identify and measure standards.

Budgeting for Talent Development

If you've ever had to defend a budget, you know how much pushback is possible. When managers think about decreasing their operating budget to create funding for employee development initiatives, they will consider it an expense. On the other hand, if managers see the many benefits of employee development, it's easier to get them to view training as an investment.

The right talent development program increases employee engagement, retention, and productivity. Ultimately, it also decreases the need for supervision, reduces absenteeism, improves customer service, lowers the number of complaints, and boosts sales. Knowledgeable employees make fewer mistakes and are more effective in dealing with customers. Providing talent development opportunities helps employees feel valued and appreciated, which makes them more committed to their work and the organization. Excellent talent development is a good investment.

Even if you are a one-person talent development shop, you will have some responsibility for preparing and maintaining the annual operating budget related to the program. You may also find yourself in charge of requesting or managing a capital budget if needed. How do you start?

Ensure You Have Commitment

Start by confirming you have full support for training efforts from senior leaders. When they understand the long-term value of employee development, they will show their support by earmarking funds for talent development.

Don't forget that employee commitment is also necessary. Give employees the data about how talent development benefits them as well as the organization, and then ask them for their input. Take a special interest in those who require certification. If they have had to invest in their own development in the past, they will be interested in the talent development program and how it will support them.

Select an Organizational Construct

You may not have a role in determining how the talent development program is organized, so understanding how it works is important. Make sure you know the source of budget funds, the reporting structure, and so forth. The five most common models are centralized, functional, matrix, university, and organization-embedded.

If you are just starting out, the model will most likely be centralized. However, if your organization decides to expand the talent development program in the future, you need to be knowledgeable about the best fit for what your organization wants to achieve. Let's look at the advantages and disadvantages of each model:

- **Centralized:** Easiest to manage; all programs, services, resources, and people are in the same location; ensures the most alignment with the organizational strategy, initiatives, metrics, delivery, and policies; generally includes a centralized budget.
- **Functional:** Combines programs and services that are related to topic areas, such as leadership or sales; most compatible with a stable organization; consistency of message across all organizational departments is the biggest concern; may create conflict of allocation of resources.
- **Matrix:** Dual reporting to both the learning department and functional departments; ensures consistency between the talent development needs of specific functions and the general learning area; drawbacks include time constraints on employees who deliver and misunderstandings of who is in charge; budget may reside in a centralized area as well as all the functional areas.
- **University:** A hybrid approach that provides access to various topics for internal and external stakeholders around values, policies, best practices, and processes within the organization, including a knowledge management platform and talent management facilities; the advantage is in the model's versatility; concerns include cost to design, broad content areas, and application accuracy; budget is located in numerous places.
- **Organization-Embedded:** Focuses on aligning business strategy, design, content, delivery, and metrics; provides a direct link from current organizational needs and strategy to daily requirements; participants are held accountable for performance; budget is usually centralized.

Create a Budget

Budgeting for talent development is usually a separate line item in an annual budget. It typically includes costs such as:

- communication about the talent development program
- delivery, such as classes, e-learning, and external course fees
- materials, such as workbooks and videos
- staff time and benefits
- administration

- purchased services
- supplies, equipment, software, and overhead
- travel and lodging if external
- assessment expenses
- design and development
- evaluation expenses.

You will need to translate your budget categories into the ones used by your organization (the finance department can help you if this is your first budget). I recommend building a relationship with the finance department, because they can help even the most seasoned practitioners translate a budget into a format that resonates with senior leaders.

Where Do the Figures Come From?

You will need to estimate costs for now—especially if this is your first talent development startup. Carolyn Nilson (2002) suggests that you begin with these seven steps:

1. Learn what line managers need and get their support.
2. Identify priorities, establish objectives, and get agreement from line managers on milestones, costs, dates, and deliverables.
3. Create the plan to achieve each objective.
4. Forecast the cost necessary to complete the plan in the time allotted by benchmarking other developmental events and other organizations.
5. Present the budget for approval.
6. Maintain records of time, salaries, materials, and other expenses so that you have a good measure next time.
7. Evaluate the budget regularly and communicate progress and problems to those who can be helpful.

PRO TIP

Be realistic right from the start, and stay honest and candid when you communicate progress. Keep the lines of communication open. No one likes surprises—especially when they're bad news about money.

The actual cost of each talent development service depends on the delivery method, how much design is required, and the content. It will vary widely. The list in Table 3-1 list offers a sample of ways that you might plan to deliver content.

Table 3-1. Relative Cost of Employee Development

Delivery Mechanism	Level of Cost
On-the-job coaching and mentoring	Low
Apprentice sponsorship	Low
Self-organized learning	Low
Videos and YouTube	Low
Paper or electronic job aids	Low
Job shadowing	Low
Facilitating teams to learn together	Low
Social learning	Low
Individual development plans (IDPs)	Low to Moderate
Online communities of practice	Moderate
E-learning programs or webcasts	Moderate
Seminars	Moderate
One-on-one tutoring	Moderate
Custom-designed programs (internal)	Moderate
Podcasts and apps	Moderate
Custom-designed programs (supplier)	High
College courses	Very High

What's a Reasonable Budget?

Organizations may establish a norm to invest a specified amount (perhaps anywhere from 2 to 8 percent of salary). Benchmark other organizations to learn what is typical for your industry. Whether the industry standard is realistic or not, it's important to name a budget the organization can commit to. You will likely have more requirements than the budget can support; however, do not reduce quality for quantity. Implement the best you can afford to ensure that you demonstrate results and continue to have the commitment, respect, and satisfaction of senior leaders.

Manage the Budget

Once approved, your training budget will need careful management to ensure that costs stay on track. Unforeseen events can lead to changing costs. For example, a specially trained staff member might unexpectedly leave the company before passing on knowledge to others. Training costs will increase if you need to rely on external resources.

Eventually your leadership will want a cost-benefit analysis—perhaps not if you are just starting, but eventually. Tracking the costs and benefits derived from developing employees adds legitimacy to the talent development program and garners respect for what you do. (Cost-benefit analysis is discussed in chapter 5.)

Can You Shave Costs?

Depending on the size of your organization and its requirements, you may find that costs add up quickly. Here are a few ways you can save on costs:

- When employees attend external learning events, ask for group discounts. Or, only send one employee, and have that person present to the rest of the staff.
- Negotiate free or reduced-cost training from suppliers for repeat business.
- Reuse materials (such as videos) and encourage staff to develop blogs or podcasts that benefit many employees.
- Utilize subject matter experts (SMEs) as much as possible to design or deliver courses.
- Encourage employees to write about or take videos of best practices, and post them in a central location for your organization.
- Identify helpful (and often free) MOOCs or online webcasts for employees to take advantage of.

However, the best way to save money in the long run is to always deliver the right content in the right way.

PRO TIP

Maintain good, no, *excellent*, records. Your budget will thank you, and your senior leader team will respect you.

Managing a Talent Development Department

Thousands of resources exist for being a better manager. Managing a talent development department incorporates the same components. In addition to what we've discussed about working with leadership and creating a budget, you'll need to consider a few additional elements—especially if you are starting a new effort.

Identify Your Team

Will you hire additional staff from the outside, or does the current pool of talent in your organization have the skills necessary? Will you depend on subject matter experts, and do you have a plan to select, manage, and reward them?

TOOLS

If you lead a small department, or if you are a one-person shop for your organization, you'll have some special challenges. The tool "10 Tips to Triumph: A Checklist for New and Small Talent Departments" is located at the end of this chapter.

Select a Learning Management System (LMS)

A good LMS can be a huge time-saver for tracking employee attendance and evaluations, as well as distributing materials. Some LMSs are also capable of delivering online training. Many resources are available to help you sort through the details to find the best one for you. Stacy Lindenberg, facilitator of ATD's Essentials of Selecting and Implementing an LMS, suggests a five-step systematic approach:

1. **Research.** Use independent research to educate your team on the strengths and weaknesses of potential suppliers. This will help narrow your selection.

2. **Peer interviews.** Talk with others in organizations similar to yours. Asking questions regarding their experience with their current LMS, as well as what they would do differently, will give you a better idea of what suppliers might be a better fit for your organization. It can also yield insight you wouldn't find otherwise.

3. **System checklists.** During the RFP and selection process, use a thoughtful and thorough checklist to compare standard features and functionality between potential suppliers.

4. **Internal advisory council.** By tapping into other areas of your organization that may be affected by the LMS, you can create a group to advise and offer insight on the LMS selection. People are also more likely to support what they have helped create, and when they have had the opportunity to provide input.

5. **Sandbox site.** When you have narrowed your selection, have your advisory council explore the supplier's sample site, often referred to as a sandbox site. This allows you and your council to use the system as users and administrators, and helps you understand system usability (Lindenberg 2012).

RESOURCES

I've found two websites that provide information about specific systems that will be helpful as you begin your search:
- Software Advice (www.softwareadvice.com/lms/#top-products)
- Software Insider (lms.softwareinsider.com).

ATD also offers a *TD at Work* issue, "Selecting and Implementing an LMS" and a book, *LMS Guidebook: Learning Management Systems Demystified.*

Note that some LMSs have come under fire recently for not actually recording "learning"—only the activity. For example, the LMS can track whether someone attended a course, but not what (if anything) was actually learned. In addition, it does not record self-organized learning, unless the employee inputs the information.

Some alternatives to the LMS include portals or intranet sites with on-demand materials that are easy to access. Some organizations also create their own organizational YouTube platform because videos are a popular learning method.

Enterprise social networks (ESNs), such as Yammer or Jive, foster collaboration and communication among peers. They provide real-time information flow, including private messaging, group formation, file storage, and often polling tools. These features allow employees to continue conversations after an event, so that learning becomes a continuous social experience.

RESOURCES

Visit www.yammer.com to learn more about Yammer; find more information about Jive at www.jivesoftware.com.

Consider Related Infrastructure Elements

If you are initiating a new, from-the-ground-up talent development effort, there is a good chance that you lack some basic infrastructure. Consider whether these systems and tools are in place, and if not, when you might use them and how you will budget for them.

- **Learning content management system.** Similar to an LMS, an LCMS also has the ability to be a platform to store and even create online learning programs.
- **HR information and performance management system.** This system uses employee data and appraisal information to help determine development needs and identify high potentials; it also uses other data to help target learning and communicate learning opportunities.
- **Design and development tools.** This can include a wide range of things, such as authoring tools to develop online courses, video production equipment, a social learning platform (such as Yammer or SharePoint), or assessment platforms to measure gains in skills or provide 360-degree feedback.
- **Talent development tools.** Beyond training events, you will want systems that allow you to easily create, store, and tap into IDPs; match mentors to protégés; and align competencies to components of the talent development program.

Of course, you can't do it all at the beginning, but review your strategic plan and decide when you might want to incorporate any of these systems into your talent development program.

Define the Rationale for Make or Buy Decisions

A big part of your time will be to secure the services and products your organize needs. In almost all cases, you will need to determine whether to use internal or external resources:

- **Internal resources.** What resources do you have in-house? Seasoned employees may be perfect to take on coaching or mentoring roles, and they're generally inexpensive to provide.
- **External resources.** What formal classes, conferences, or certification efforts are required? These may be more expensive, but are professionally developed and often yield good results.

Whether you make or buy services and products, your decision has numerous repercussions. You will need to consider cost, alignment to the organization, internal expertise, ability to customize the content, time available, speed with which it is needed, how often the product or service will be needed, production technology, credibility of the supplier, and others. You will most likely use a combination of internal and external resources during your tenure. Table 3-2 can help you make your decision.

Table 3-2. Define the Rationale for Make or Buy Decisions

Use Internal Resources	Use External Resources
• Qualified and credible experts are available • Specific knowledge is only available internally • Building credibility with sponsors is desired • There is time to guide SMEs • Time is available to test products and services • Budget constraints exist • An experienced instructional designer and organization development expert are available • Quality materials can be produced quickly and inexpensively • Relevant data are only available internally • A "mistrust of not-invented-here" mentality exists in the organization	• The best expertise is available outside the organization • An objective or fresh perspective is required • Time is of the essence • Staff are not available to dedicate time to the project • Budget is available • The organization lacks the technology or ability to produce superior materials • Relevant, credible materials and programs are available • Customization is not required • Outside authorities have more credibility

Besides these critical considerations, additional things to include would be updating or changing the organization's employee handbook, writing job descriptions, determining a pay structure, creating a staff development plan, and other actions you would want to address by researching or tapping into your past experiences.

RESOURCES

The *TD at Work* issue "Managing Learning Programs Step by Step" by Lisa Downs provides a list of questions for overcoming obstacles and a section for how to secure executive buy-in and support.

Identifying Topics Employees Need to Learn

How do you know what topics or content to deliver? Earlier in this chapter, we examined how to connect learning to the organizational strategy. That gives you a big-picture view of needs. You'll determine your content by conducting needs assessments and analyzing them. You've already looked at the organizational level; however, because needs assessments occur at three levels—organizational, task, and individual—you will also conduct needs assessment with managers and perhaps even employees.

A needs assessment usually occurs at the start of a training cycle so you can determine needs or gaps between the current and the desired result. It generally refers to a gap in employee performance, but that does not necessarily mean that training is the solution. A needs assessment is your path to clarify problems and determine the best way to close the gap. For example, a needs assessment in human performance improvement helps you determine the needs related to performance issues, and may uncover a broad variety of topics, such as processes, resources, and organizational structures.

How do you conduct a needs assessment? If you've completed the activities in previous chapters, you've already conducted a type of needs assessment. There are a variety of approaches—including interviews, observations, questionnaires, performance data reviews, focus groups, and knowledge tests—that can lead to identifying needs. Using them effectively involves gathering, analyzing, verifying, and reporting data. So, when you interviewed leaders and managers, you were conducting a needs assessment from the organizational perspective.

TOOLS

The six data collection approaches listed in the "Data Collection Approaches" tool in chapter 5 can be used to gather data for a needs assessment as well as evaluation.

A needs assessment may serve several purposes:

- It places the need or request in the context of the organization's needs. Training or employee development adds value when it serves a business need.

- It validates or dispels any initial issues presented by a manager or leader. Although managers and clients know the business, sometimes they don't know the cause of or the remedy for issues that involve human performance.
- It ensures that the ultimate learning design supports employee performance and thereby helps the organization meet its needs.
- It results in recommendations regarding nontraining issues that may be interfering with the achievement of desired organization and employee goals.
- It establishes the foundation for evaluation.

TOOLS

The "Needs Assessment Process" tool briefly lists the steps required to complete a needs assessment; it is located at the end of this chapter.

As mentioned, a needs assessment occurs at three different levels:

- Organizational assessment evaluates the level of organizational performance. It may determine the skills, knowledge, and attitude needs of an organization to achieve its strategic imperative. It also identifies what is required to alleviate organizational problems and weaknesses, as well as enhance strengths and competencies. Organizational assessments consider factors such as changing demographics, political trends, technology, or the economy.
- Task assessment examines the skills, knowledge, and attitudes required for specific jobs and occupational groups. It identifies how and which discrepancies or gaps exist, as well as new ways to do work that could prevent discrepancies or close the gaps.
- Individual assessment analyzes how well an individual employee is doing a job and determines the individual's capacity to do new or different work. It provides information about which employees need training and what kind (Biech 2017).

TOOLS

The "Plan Your Needs Assessment" tool gives you a list of questions to help design your needs assessment.

A needs assessment will be helpful for you to decide whether talent development is the solution or if others need to be pulled in to find the best resolution. For example, if someone comes to you and says, "We need training. Half of my employees are not meeting their goals." You need to consider more than employee skills and knowledge. Do they have the physical resources, tools, and technology they need? Are the processes, reporting relationships, incentives, and consequences appropriate for the work? Are employees motivated and healthy enough to perform the task? Talent development professionals need to be performance consultants and good communicators to determine the root cause of a situation. The solution may be in the talent development arena, such as training, coaching, or job-aid creation, but it also might lie in a business department's processes, HR's policies, or even the organization's misdirected strategic guidance.

Remember, just because someone has requested training doesn't mean that training is required. It means that something needs attention. The needs assessment will help determine whether training is the solution.

Reinforce a Mindset That Supports Today's Learner

Malcolm Knowles' work was never more relevant than it is today. We can summarize his principles of adult learning by saying that adults are self-directed, have an extensive depth of experience, are ready to learn more, and are goal motivated (1984). Keep these principles in mind as we review several other concepts that support how learners want to learn in ways that Knowles could never have imagined.

Our organizations are changing, and the most productive and valuable employees are changing with them. To be productive, employees need to be prepared for the VUCA world in which their organizations operate. This means that talent development professionals' jobs are changing, too.

"Meet the Modern Learner," an infographic by Bersin by Deloitte, received lots of attention when it was published in 2014. Based on research conducted throughout the year, the infographic presents valuable advice to consider as you think of how to meet the needs of your learners. For example:

RESOURCES
You can retrieve a copy of the "Meet the Modern Learner" infographic at http://bit.ly/2wlUPih.

- "Most learners won't watch videos longer than four minutes"; therefore, learning experiences need to be presented in short, microbursts.
- Employees check their phones nine times an hour and are "increasingly turning to their smartphones to find just-in-time answers to unexpected problems"; therefore, learning needs to be on the go and on demand.
- Employees are looking for "pull" learning (continuous, shared, and available).
- Employees want to learn but are overwhelmed with work, and only "38 percent feel they have access to learning and growth at work"; therefore, learning needs to be more aligned with work, and organizations need to find ways to incorporate learning and provide opportunities for self-organized learning.
- "Employees want to learn from their peers and managers as much as from experts"; therefore, ensure that social and continuous development is available (Tauber and Johnson 2014).

An Organizational Learning Culture Is Required

Herb Kelleher, co-founder, former CEO, and now chairman emeritus of Southwest Airlines, is fond of saying, "Culture is what people do when no one is looking." Culture and engagement are often cited as the "very important" challenges senior leaders face as well as being critical to business success (Derler 2016; Aguirre, von Post, and Alpern 2013).

The 70-20-10 Principle Guides Development

As talent development professionals, we have focused on the 10 percent—formal learning. It's clear that we need to become more adept at supporting and enhancing the 90 percent that occurs beyond the classroom. We need to get better at putting learning where the work is, ensuring that the right developmental activities are available at the right time.

Managers Are Responsible for Employee Development

A good manager is one who takes developing employees seriously. Developing employees for the job they are doing is a start, but star managers develop employees for their next jobs. They ensure that learning continues by helping employees learn how to learn. The managers who are the most successful ensure that every employee has an IDP and builds in time for regularly scheduled discussions about their IDPs.

Enlightened Employees Take Responsibility for Their Own Development

It took the Millennial generation to show the rest of us the value of being accountable for your own development. More and more employees recognize that they need to take control of skill development. The Bersin infographic shows us that rapid organizational changes mean everyone needs to constantly be learning. When employees do not get training and development from their employers, they find other options—including paying for it themselves.

Talent Development Professionals Need Consulting Skills

One last mindset is that consulting skills are critical to your work as an internal talent development professional. We do not have the pages to address this topic by itself, but you will find elements of it throughout this book. You will need to use consulting skills to identify problems and create solutions. You may also need them when you are performance consulting, leading a development strategy, building teams, weighing in on organizational change, and for what you are about to do right now—starting a talent development program. Indeed, this book's philosophy is based on using internal consulting skills.

RESOURCES

Two excellent resources for the consulting efforts of your talent development program are:

- *Consulting on the Inside* by Beverly Scott and B. Kim Barnes
- *Flawless Consulting* by Peter Block.

If your focus is on performance, read *Performance Consulting: A Strategic Process to Improve, Measure, and Sustain Organizational Results* by Dana Gaines Robinson and four other authors.

These five mindsets prepare you for designing and delivering a learning strategy that supports today's learner and today's organization.

Your Strategy Is in Place

With a talent development strategy in hand and your operating plan established, you have the key logistics in place. This allows you to begin thinking about how you can best deliver services for your organization. The next chapter provides a guide for how to plan for services and how to determine content that will be critical for your organization to achieve its strategy.

Questions to Explore

- What is the best way to conduct research for creating a talent development strategic plan for your organization?
- What are the key benefits of creating a business case for a talent development program?
- What are your concerns about writing your talent development strategic plan?
- Who could assist you to complete a SWOT analysis?
- If you decide to conduct interviews, what questions will you ask?
- What will you include in your policy statement?
- What have you identified to include in your budget? Who can you call in your network to help you with your first budgeting drill?
- What issues do you predict regarding the budget?
- What are the most important considerations when deciding whether you will develop learning internally or use external resources?
- What learner mindsets will pose the greatest challenge for you?

Tools for Support

Explore Your Organization's Strategic Priorities

Use this template as a guide to identify your organization's strategic priorities. If you have the option to work with a team, it will lead to richer data and more insight.

- If you are not familiar with your organization or if you have joined a new one, read about the organization and the industry. Start on the Internet, move to industry journals, and ask for other resource recommendations from leaders. How are your leaders rewarded? How does this compare with the industry standard?
- Learn about your organization's customers and what they expect. Read your latest customer surveys. Check online to see what ratings your customers are giving your organization. Discuss what you learn with leaders you respect.
- Interview leaders. Create a list of questions that address not only what is happening now, but also what their hopes and dreams are for the organization's future.
- Learn what employees think about the organization. Read at least the last two engagement surveys. Is the organization getting better or worse? In what areas?
- Read your organization's strategic plan. What are its priorities? By when? What resources are going to be needed? What skills, knowledge, and attitudes are necessary?
- Learn about your organization's culture. What values are advocated? What values actually play out? What is rewarded? How is learning viewed? How is change managed?

Mind Map Priorities

A mind map is a useful tool to identify what knowledge, skills, and attitudes are necessary to address the strategic priorities. It is a diagram—often created around a single topic—that helps you visually organize information by giving it a hierarchy and showing how one piece relates to the whole. Tony Buzan, a British popular psychology author and TV personality who popularized the term *mind map*, describes them as, "a powerful graphic technique which provides a universal key to unlock the potential of the brain. It harnesses the full range of cortical skills—word, image, number, logic, rhythm, colour and spatial awareness—in a single, uniquely powerful manner. In so doing, it gives you the freedom to roam the infinite expanses of your brain" (Buzan 2011).

The beauty of the mind map is that it is a way for you to capture ideas in one place, and then creatively explore and expand options for the content of the design.

Place each of your organization's priorities in the center of a mind map and start identifying what your employees will need to achieve the priorities. Take the mind map to any departments that are primarily and secondarily related to each priority for additional input.

SWOT Analysis

Use this tool to complete a SWOT analysis to help you prepare to develop your talent development strategy.

	Positives	Downsides
Internal	Strengths	Weaknesses
External	Opportunities	Threats

Interview Questions to Ask

Choose your questions carefully when interviewing senior leaders or others during the pre-implementation stage. A 45-minute, one-on-one interview will provide enough information.

Use these questions to get started. You will want to tailor them to your organization and your audience. Begin every interview with a short description of the purpose and how the content of the discussion will be used. If anonymity is important, state your intentions.

- ❑ Tell me about your experience with employee development.
- ❑ What kinds of employee development tactics work best from your perspective?
- ❑ What are the top three things we should consider when developing a talent development program?
- ❑ How does the organization's culture either support or inhibit employee development? What can we do to either strengthen the support or weaken the inhibitors?
- ❑ Which organizational strategies need support from a talent development program? How?
- ❑ What knowledge and skills do employees in the organization (your department, division, unit) need? What are your ideas for delivering specific skills and knowledge?
- ❑ In your mind, what should the organization invest in for its talent development program?
- ❑ What are your top three priorities for the talent development program?
- ❑ What message would you give the CEO (or vice presidents, managers, supervisors, and employees) about our new talent development program?
- ❑ What commitment and accountability will be necessary for a successful talent development program?
- ❑ Talent development is everyone's responsibility. What role do you envision playing in the talent development program?
- ❑ Who else should I interview?
- ❑ Is there anything that I should have asked, but didn't? Anything you wanted to tell me that I did not give you a chance to say?

Strategic Planning Template

Use this template to guide writing your strategic plan for talent development.

Executive Summary

(I recommend that you write this last.)

Background and Context

- Why this strategy now?
    » organizational context
    » learning function context
    » political, economic, social, and technological analysis
    » SWOT analysis
    » areas transitioning from weakness to strength.
- Who we are:
    » our vision
    » our mission
    » our learning philosophy or principles
    » how do the above align with the direction of the organization we serve?
- Who we serve:
    » our primary clients
    » key partners
    » stakeholders.
- How we serve:
    » our business model
    » product portfolio
    » service portfolio
    » key services provided by others
    » organizational structure
    » financial model, especially as it touches the customer.
- Where we are going:
    » strategic goals
    » systemic goals
    » programmatic goals.

- How we will get there:
  - » our key strategies and initiatives
  - » year 1
  - » year 2
  - » year 3
  - » year 4
  - » year 5.
  - » our requirements for:
    - ♦ political support
    - ♦ data
    - ♦ financial support
    - ♦ physical and virtual space
    - ♦ technology
    - ♦ indicators of success.
- Broad-based measures of success:
  - » how will we demonstrate:
    - ♦ effectiveness
    - ♦ efficiency
    - ♦ quality.
- Year 1 design

Used with permission from Coné (2014).

Aligning Employee Development to Organizational Strategy

Use this checklist to generate ideas and remind yourself and others to maintain focus on the organizational strategy when making decisions about training and development.

- ❏ Target talent development budget increases to specific business goals.
- ❏ Make sure any university or educational programs support the organization's strategic plan.
- ❏ Evaluate the impact talent development efforts have on the strategy.
- ❏ Align performance to strategy.
- ❏ Define the "why" as the achievement of business outcomes first.
- ❏ Create effective governance mechanisms linking the business to talent development.
- ❏ Meet regularly with line managers to identify their needs and issues.
- ❏ Ask the line managers lots of questions.
- ❏ Become a trusted adviser using Dana Gaines Robinson's ACT model (access, credibility, trust) with business leaders.
- ❏ Know how to diagnose business issues.
- ❏ Communicate regularly and build a relationship with line managers.
- ❏ Ensure learning is co-owned between talent development and the business.
- ❏ Ensure personal and 360-degree assessments have a strong focus on strategy.
- ❏ Implement action learning projects that relate to the organization's strategy.
- ❏ Create development goals that relate to strategy.

Talent Development Policy Template

Use this template and sample stem statements as prompts to start writing the three key parts of your talent development policy: the value statement, belief statement, and action statement.

Value Statement

- We value . . .
- Our mission is to . . .
- To support the organization's strategy, we will strive to . . .
- We will uphold . . .

Belief Statement

- We will maintain the organization's belief that . . .
- We believe that . . .
- To fulfill the organization's mission, we will . . .

Action Statement

- To accomplish our goals, we will . . .
- It is mandatory that we . . .
- We will partner with the organization's leaders to . . .

Example of a Simplified Talent Development Policy

This simplified version of a training policy provides examples of the wording you might consider.

The talent development department's mission is to partner with the business units to ensure all employees have the knowledge, skills, and attitudes to create a competitive advantage. We value integrity, innovation, and teamwork. *(value statement)*

The talent development department believes that the employees of the organization are its most valuable asset. Working together with the business units will allow us to create excellent products for all customers. We believe it is essential that all employees acquire the knowledge and skills necessary to perform their jobs at the highest level possible. We believe that people learn in three ways: formally, on the job, and socially. *(belief statement)*

The talent development department believes that success is incumbent on these actions: *(action statement)*

- All levels of management will be involved in planning talent development efforts.
- All learning will be aligned to the organization's strategy and goals.
- New employees will receive a dynamic, informative, and interactive orientation to the organization.
- All managers will be given the tools and support to develop their employees.
- Using the 70-20-10 model as a guide, we will support, encourage, and deliver services and products to ensure employees learn continuously.
- All employees will be viewed as leaders of the organization and given the skills and knowledge to perform their responsibilities as such.
- A variety of activities, services, and deliverables will be designed to support employees who require continuous learning on demand and on the go.
- The training policy will be reviewed and updated annually to reflect changes to the organization's strategy and goals.

10 Tips to Triumph: A Checklist for New and Small Talent Departments

Being a new and small talent department presents unique challenges. Follow these guidelines and be sure not to fall into any of the traps described.

- Keep solutions, services, and products simple.
- Become business savvy.
- Don't overpromise.
- Keep all promises.
- Don't try to do everything.
- Don't try to do everything yourself.
- Remain optimistic and positive.
- Maintain your own development.
- Attend your association's annual conference every year.
- Take care of yourself—so you can take care of your organization.

Needs Assessment Process

This tool will help you start developing a needs assessment and lead you to implementation.

1. Draft questions you will ask.
2. Solicit feedback for the questions from stakeholders or other colleagues.
3. Identify the approach you will use, such as interviews or questionnaires, to gather data. (See the list in the chapter 5 tools.)
4. Conduct the assessment.
5. Analyze and compile the data.
6. Determine if the results identify a talent development solution.
   » If yes, continue to step 7.
   » If no, deliver the results to the correct stakeholder and offer to help.
7. Create an implementation plan.
   » Establish goals, which are most likely based on the gaps or needs you discover.
   » Compare the results with your organization's competency model.
   » Create learning objectives.
   » Decide what methodology you will use, such as training, supervisory coaching, a job aid, review of information, or peer groups.
   » Decide who should receive the solution, when, and how it will be delivered.
   » Determine if you have the resources to design the solution or if you will require an external supplier.
   » Create an evaluation plan.
8. Connect with business leaders to communicate your ideas and involve them in the solution.
9. Finalize the design and development.
10. Communicate the talent development solution throughout the organization.
11. Implement the talent development solution.

Plan Your Needs Assessment

Consider these questions as you plan your needs assessment.

- Who is being trained? What are their job functions?
- Are employees from the same department or a variety of areas or locations in the organization?
- What are the deficiencies? Why has this occurred?
- What are the backgrounds and educational profiles of the employees being studied?
- What do employees expect or desire?
- What are the objectives of the needs assessment?
- How will the results of the needs assessment benefit the organization?
- What are the expected outcomes? What effect will these outcomes have on which organizational levels?
- Which data gathering method will work best: questionnaires, surveys, tests, interviews?
- Who will administer the assessment—in-house or external consultants?
- Will the analysis interrupt work processes? What effect will this have on the workforce and productivity?
- How will you measure success?
- How is the request tied to the organizational strategy?
- What is the organizational climate?
- Will there be a confidentiality policy for handling information?

Used with permission from Biech (2017).

References and Additional Resources

Aguirre, D., R. von Post, and M. Alpern. 2013. *Culture's Role in Enabling Organizational Change.* Booz & Company. www.strategyand.pwc.com/reports/cultures-role -organizational-change.

ASTD and i4cp (American Society for Training & Development and the Institute for Corporate Productivity). 2012. *Developing Results: Aligning Learning's Goals and Outcomes With Business Performance Measures.* Alexandria, VA: ASTD Press.

Barbazette, J. 2008. *Managing the Training Function for Bottom Line Results.* San Francisco: Pfeiffer.

Bianco-Mathis, V., and L.K. Nabors. 2016. "Building a Coaching Organization." *TD at Work.* Alexandria, VA: ATD Press.

Biech, E. 2017. *The Art and Science of Training.* Alexandria, VA: ATD Press.

———. 2016. "The 90% Solution." *TD*, December.

———. 2009a. *10 Steps to Successful Training.* Alexandria, VA: ASTD Press.

———. 2009b. "Learning Eye to Eye: Aligning Training to Business Objectives." *T+D* 60 (4): 50.

Block, P. 2011. *Flawless Consulting: A Guide to Getting Your Expertise Used,* 3rd edition. San Francisco: Pfeiffer.

Buzan, T. 2011. "What Is a Mind Map?" Mind Mapping | Tony Buzan. www.tonybuzan.com/about/mind-mapping.

Coné, J. 2014. "Developing a Strategy for Training and Development." Chapter 42 in *ASTD Handbook: The Definitive Reference for Training & Development,* 2nd ed., Edited by E. Biech. Alexandria, VA: ASTD Press.

Derler, A. 2016. *High-Impact Leadership: The New Leadership Maturity Model.* Bersin by Deloitte.

Downs, L. 2015. "Managing Learning Programs Step by Step." *TD at Work.* Alexandria, VA: ATD Press.

Edwards, L. 2014. "Creating an Internal Coaching Program." *TD at Work.* Alexandria, VA: ATD Press.

Haddock-Millar, J., and D. Clutterbuck. 2016. "5 Critical Conversations to Talent Development." *TD at Work.* Alexandria, VA: ATD Press.

Knowles, M. 1984. *Andragogy in Action.* San Francisco, CA: Josey-Bass.

Lindenberg, S. 2012. "Selecting and Implementing an LMS." *Infoline.* Alexandria, VA: ASTD Press.

Neal, B. 2014. "How to Develop Training Quality Standards." *Infoline.* Alexandria, VA: ASTD Press.

Nilson, C. 2002. *How to Start a Training Program.* Alexandria, VA: ASTD Press.

Reinhold, D., T. Patterson, and P. Hegel. 2015. *Make Learning Stick: Best Practices to Get the Most Out of Leadership Development.* Greensboro, NC: Center for Creative Leadership.

Robinson, D., J.C. Robinson, J.J. Phillips, P.P. Phillips, and D. Handshaw. 2015. *Performance Consulting: A Strategic Process to Improve, Measure, and Sustain Organizational Results,* 3rd edition. Oakland, CA: Berrett-Koehler.

Scisco, P., E. Biech, and G. Hallenbeck. 2017. *Compass: Your Guide for Leadership Development and Coaching.* Greensboro, NC: Center for Creative Leadership.

Schlenker, B. 2015. "Back to the Future . . . of Training and Development." Session given at the ATD International Conference & Exposition, Orlando, FL, May 2015.

Scott, B., and B.K. Barnes. 2011. *Consulting on the Inside: A Practical Guide for Internal Consultants.* Alexandria, VA: ASTD Press.

Tauber, T., and D. Johnson. 2014. "Meet the Modern Learner." Infographic. Bersin by Deloitte. www.bersin.com/Lib/Rs/ShowDocument.aspx?docid=18071.

4

Implementing the Plan: How Do You Execute an Effective Talent Development Program?

In This Chapter

- Delivery options and decisions based on 70-20-10
- Exploring possible services the talent development professional could offer
- Post-implementation steps
- Roll-out plans

I t's tempting to put off starting a talent development program indefinitely, waiting until there is more time or more money. But for an organization to succeed, it must have competent, engaged, developed employees. As you saw in previous chapters, skilled employees can help an organization grow and prosper. Employee development is one of the most important investments an organization can make in its future.

The steps you took in chapter 3 flow directly into the decisions required to execute your talent development program. The strategic decisions, or the "how," make it easier to decide what to incorporate into the design. You might consider chapter 4 as how, part 2.

Implementation in this What Works book may be a bit different from other books in this series. Other topics focus implementation on the *I* in ADDIE—implementing the onboarding session or the first blended learning course or a new compliance training program. You can probably imagine that starting a talent development program—a larger, more complex effort—will be slightly different.

Implementation for starting a talent development program focuses on the decisions you incorporate into the final plan. What instructor-led classes will we offer? What is talent development's role in on-the-job learning? How can we support "learning from others" in person or through social networks? What services shall we offer departments and managers to ensure employees are developed efficiently and effectively?

Design Planning for Executing a Talent Development Program

And now the fun begins! It may seem as if you have been planning and planning to get to this point. It's true, but all that planning has put you in a good place to make the decisions required to implement and execute a talent development program. If you've followed the plan I've outlined so far, you now know:

- what your leaders expect and how they will evaluate the program
- how talent development supports the organization's strategy
- what managers need
- what your talent development strategy will be.

You've also conducted a needs assessment to ensure that the problem can be resolved using a talent development approach.

The Needs Assessment

Your needs assessment helped identify the skills and competencies in which employees are least proficient. It also probably highlighted common learning needs and problems across the organization. Your needs assessment may have been a very simple listing, where employees selected the top requirements, or you may have observed employees and recorded their needs. Or perhaps you conducted a more complex gap analysis or discussed needs with managers and leaders. The needs assessment also identified who needs training by groups or segments or individuals.

At any rate, you probably have uncovered more requirements than the budget can deliver. Therefore, you will need to prioritize the needs. For example, higher priorities may depend on the content and organization's needs, or even topics that have the broadest impact. Lower-priority needs may include a smaller group of employees or may be less critical to the organization's goals.

PRO TIP

Create a decision matrix to make prioritizing development needs easier. You could include criteria such as safety, risk reduction, urgent, morale, retention, engagement, senior leader expectations, innovation, competition, and other measures that may be important to your organization.

Ideally, the best strategic development plan is the sweet spot of where the organization's and individual's needs and desires overlap (Figure 4-1). The organization is interested in managing succession, filling its leadership pipeline, and achieving its strategic imperative. Employees are interested in managing their careers, improving performance, and developing skills. When the desired competencies and development needs come together, everyone wins.

Figure 4-1. Overlap of Organizational and Individual Development Needs

Organization

- Manage succession
- Fill the leadership pipeline
- Operate effectively and efficiently
- Achieve its strategic imperative

Individual

- Develop skills
- Acquire knowledge
- Improve performance
- Manage career growth

Selecting Design Plan Options

You have many design and delivery strategies available to you. We won't be able to cover all of them in depth, but additional resources are listed that will help you make decisions that cannot be covered within the space in this book. Keeping your focus on organizational priorities, let's look at the plethora of possibilities for learning that are available.

We will operate from a 70-20-10 perspective—which by now you know is simply a guide to remind us that learning occurs in many ways. While in the past the focus was often on the 10 percent, formal learning, you now have the chance to implement a plan that spreads across all development opportunities and throughout the organization.

Many of the kinds of learning activities that we are about to explore could cross over into two or even all three categories. For example, following an experiential activity in a formal setting, you could plan to share contact information and organize peer accountability groups that discuss implementation ideas on the job. This section is not about disputing which category is better, but more to present all the options for you to consider. Learning doesn't stop and start again; learners move from one activity to another—they all blend together to form a well-developed employee. Most important for you is to consider how activities from all three areas can work together.

No matter what kind of learning methodology you are planning, remember the visual presented in chapter 3 (Figure 4-2). It is a reminder that learning should link to the business strategy—either directly or indirectly to support general employee growth and development. An example of that would be general communication. Everyone needs to be the best communicator possible.

Figure 4-2. Linking Learner Development to Business Goals

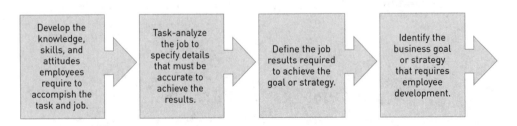

Because you are just starting out, you have a blank slate. Later on, you may have many more decisions to make to determine the best way to budget your time and resources. You want to do a great job. The funny thing is, the better job you do, the busier you become!

What to Consider for Formal Learning—10 Percent

We discussed a number of learning events in chapter 1 that are included in this category. Let's expand on the delivery options here, and consider how to select content for formal learning.

Delivery Options

What delivery options are available? Instructor-led training in both the traditional classroom and virtual classroom, professional accreditations—such as college degrees, certification, or apprenticeships—and self-directed or self-organized learning are all possible. Others that you might not think of include reading, independent research, and even casual events you might deliver, such as lunch & learn events or guest speakers who have been invited to your organization. And you may also want to determine how MOOCs fit into your talent development plans.

Remember that there will be crossover in the kinds of events that could be classified as part of the 70, 20, or 10 categories. Many criteria come into play. We mentioned some when discussing budgets in the last chapter. This is not about memorizing an "approved list." It is more important that:

- You consider all options as a part of your strategy.
- You determine what works best in your organization.
- When you specify content, you determine a good match to the methodology you select.
- You decide upon the best choice for the learner. What will be the most effective and efficient process available? Remember, it's all about the learner.

We can examine the options one step deeper. For example, you have choices of one-on-one versus group sessions, e-learning versus in-person instruction, on-site or off-site, canned or customized, internal trainer or consultant. Can it be mobile? Your answers will be determined by a combination of factors: what's available, what best suits your needs, what platform and equipment you and your learners have available, and what you have in your budget. The number one decision criterion is what the organization needs.

Delivery Support

What happens prior to and follows the training event are equally critical to success. You can support the delivery using workbooks, participant manuals, job aids, models, checklists, follow-up help sessions; by getting supervisors involved; or by encouraging learning partners or communities of practice. You may not know what is necessary as you develop the strategy, but add a placeholder in your design so that you remember what to include.

TOOLS

"Sometimes All You Need Is a Job Aid" is a tool at the end of chapter 6 that will help you identify the best job aid to use in various situations.

Designing to Meet Business Requirements

As a trusted adviser to your leaders, you have an opportunity to educate management and provide data that support your rationale. Take the following steps to ensure the formal learning events you design and develop link to organizational goals:

- If you haven't already, review all relevant documentation, such as corporate strategic and business plans, and if the training is linked to a specific department, the departmental business plans.
- Interview the leaders of departments that have requested training to clarify the problems they are trying to solve.
- If formal events are already available either internally or externally, discuss how they are aligned to and support an organizational requirement.
- Be alert to future changes your organization is facing, and anticipate the kind of support it will need.
- Frame your questions to be certain that you have considered the issues of aligning formal learning to organizational goals and strategy.

TOOLS

The "Alignment Questions to Ask While Designing Formal Learning" tool offers a few starting questions you might ask of your stakeholders as you design formal learning. You'll find it at the end of this chapter.

Talent development professionals must incorporate many tasks when designing training, including developing objectives and materials; considering instructional methods, timing, and participation; and addressing questions. They must also assess session length and cost, develop audiovisuals and experiential learning activities, create a safe learning environment, practice delivery skills, and more. So, concerns about adding "meeting business requirements"—yet another thing to remember—are understandable. Don't think of the business requirement as one more thing to do. Instead, think of it as a process that ties everything together so that you can systematically design an expanded, yet holistic learning experience.

The design doesn't begin when your participants walk in the door, and it doesn't end when they leave. It begins as soon as you identify a need and continues until you are sure the participants are contributing to the intended organizational goals. Here are a few ways you can ensure the design meets business requirements:

- Incorporate steps into your design that prepare employees for what will happen during training prior to the learning experience. These steps should include a conversation with the employees' supervisors.
- Talk to management about what the employees are expected to do differently or better, and how this aligns with business goals.
- Identify what actions management will take to support changes following the training session (including reinforcement and feedback); share these actions with participants.
- Design support—both hard copy and online materials—that can be used following the training session.
- Ensure that participants know how their efforts will affect business goals.
- Be certain that participants know what is expected of them and how they will be held accountable following the training event.
- Clearly identify the facilitator's role in support and follow-up.
- Be sure participants know how they can find assistance following the training session.

Ensuring Follow-Up and Application

Ensuring transfer of learning is possibly one of the most important and most overlooked aspects of producing successful training. Yet if you step back and think about it, this is where success is defined. Many books have been written about the "did training take?" conundrum. It is important to identify what you can do to ensure that training takes, rather than fixating later on why it didn't. Let's look at a few ways you can ensure that follow-up and application of the skills and knowledge learned in the training session are implemented:

- Follow up with managers and supervisors within 24 hours of the training session to answer questions or to goad them into action if necessary.
- Email or text participants asking what on-the-job actions they have taken since the training session.
- Review the accountability plan put in place during the design process.
- Gather data about how many participants are using the support systems (coaching, blogs, and any others) you created. Use the data to make improvements where necessary.
- Review the talent development department's role to determine the level of support that is provided and whether it is appropriate for your organization's culture.

Remember that your organization invests in training and developing its employees. Therefore, talent development should be treated like other investments—goals need to be aligned, appropriate plans made, and accountability measured.

What's in Your Implementation Plan for the 10 Percent?

What are all the possible options you may be responsible for in formal learning, commonly called the 10 percent? You will have the results of your needs assessment; a list of classes that address the needs at an organizational, task, and individual level; a plan and schedule for the design and delivery of all formal events; a calendar of events that will be rolled out to the organization; and a list of next steps.

A Word About Blended Learning

Let's consider blended learning for a minute, because it often bridges delivery methods between various ways we learn. I've written about blended learning in several other books—mostly to clarify confusion about the topic. Blended learning is a planned combination of training delivery options such as coaching, online classes, reading, breakfast with colleagues, or reference manuals.

Blended learning is not about using as many different delivery options as you can, but using the right one for the content, the learner, and the organization. Ask yourself, "What do learners need to know, and what is the best way to deliver the content?" Blended learning designs:

- Optimize resources, providing the most effect for the least investment.
- Consider what is accepted and expected by the organization.
- Stay solution-focused; that is, what is the business problem to be solved and what is the best way to solve it?
- Consider learners' needs, the time that is available, how motivated they are, and access to technology that may be necessary.
- Require that you focus on the kind of development that is needed: knowledge, skill development, or attitude changes (Biech 2015b).

Actually, I like to think of 70-20-10 as the first blended learning design.

RESOURCES

According to Jennifer Hofmann, author of *Blended Learning*, the second book in this series, "All learning is blended learning."

What to Consider for Learning From Others—20 Percent

This category is sometimes called social, self-directed, or just general informal learning. Be careful, though, when you add the phrase *social learning* to the mix; it immediately conjures up weaving people together into a social network, such as Yammer or Jive, and expecting that the experience will radically help them learn. This is certainly one way to learn from others, but it isn't the only way. I do believe that learning is "social," but I do not believe you have to always use technology to facilitate learning from others. It has its advantages, especially when learners are separated by time and location. But I don't want you to think that if your organization doesn't have the hottest new social infrastructure that you can't participate in social learning. That's not true. There are many other delivery mechanisms—like talking to one another.

Delivery Options

Your organization faces many challenges, including a shortage of talent and an expanding skills gap. Talent development professionals have a unique opportunity to enhance their value to the organization by showing how we can adapt and use our skills to develop today's employees beyond the classroom. This includes on-demand or informal learning, which is often enhanced by online learning options, such as podcasts, tablet-based learning, and mobile learning. Employees can also leverage professional development opportunities.

Consider learning from others an integral part of talent development. Capturing perspectives from internal and external colleagues, in real time, enables the informal learning environment. And it is growing every day. According to the report *Informal Learning: The Social Revolution*, from ATD and i4cp (2013), 27 percent of respondents stated that more than half of their learning was done informally. And the actual number is probably higher. It's difficult to estimate informal learning because most of us are oblivious to the fact that we are actually learning during conversations with colleagues.

It takes a team to create a social media plan for your organization. Talent development professionals can help organizations by coordinating with other department such as IT and legal. You can take the lead by learning what social media are currently used, how, why, and who owns the processes. IT will be interested in security and technical issues, and will also help with archiving and deployment. Legal will help with approval strategies and guidance for sensitive corporate knowledge, processes, or practices, as well as reporting requirements. You have expertise in learning tools, cultural readiness, community management, and what employees need to learn.

Talent development professionals help employees learn from others in several ways, including establishing systems channels to easily request peer feedback in a one-on-one setting or from many in a peer accountability group. Learners may be engaged as a mentor or protégé in a traditional arrangement, a reverse mentoring scenario, or a peer mentoring group. We can help employees locate and learn from blogs, wikis, or online professional communities, such as those at ATD or on LinkedIn. The 360-degree feedback process is great a way for them to learn from others. You can connect learners through social media by using discussion boards, incorporating Twitter feeds, and sharing content on Facebook. You can enable watercooler learning by emailing a question of the day to an employee group. In addition, the social aspect of gaming can enhance problem-solving skills, because it is experiential and provides a way to share personal and professional experiences.

TOOLS

The tool "Fifteen Quick Ways to Continue to Learn From Others," located at the end of this chapter, will spark your own creative ideas to encourage employees to learn from one another.

Delivery Support

How can you support employees? One way is to make it easy to establish a community of practice. Find ways your organization can use technology to share information for immediate use. Remember, however, that the true value is using the information to build skills, knowledge, and attitudes for the long run.

It is important to learn about your organization's policies for using social media, so you know what boundaries exist. You may be able to adjust them to be more user friendly where necessary, depending on your organization. If increased mobile learning is in your company's future, get involved with figuring out how to make it work for everyone.

What's Your Role in Helping Employees Learn From Others?

Your role is not about designing and delivering training. Instead, it is about helping learners create methods to learn from one another. Consider having learners curate the content so that it is available anywhere at any time—just remember that this might require you to establish a taxonomy and curation plan. Other responsibilities may include organizing accountability relationships, establishing mentor-protégé relationships, identifying coaches, helping others utilize apps and mobile learning, connecting learners through social media, inspiring feedback, and enabling watercooler learning.

What's in Your Implementation Plan for the 20 Percent?

What items are you responsible for when employees are learning from others, commonly called the 20 percent? Your role is one of a facilitator—I like to think of it as a matchmaker role. Your implementation plan will have a list of social network tools currently available; potential research you want to do to expand social tools; a plan and schedule for informing supervisors about the benefits of informal learning; a plan for capturing and curating learning that takes place among employees; an implementation plan for mentors and protégés; initial guidance for coaching efforts; an exploratory plan for implementing a coaching effort; and plans to use discussion boards, Twitter, texts, and other tools to keep watercooler learning alive.

RESOURCES
What happens to our brains when we learn? Take a look at Lara Boyd's TEDx Talk, "After Watching This, Your Brain Will Not Be the Same," to find out (http://bit.ly/29RKdNV).

What to Consider for On-the-Job Learning— 70 Percent

This category is sometimes called practice, work flow, or assignments. Some also call it experiential, but I completely disagree with this label. Why? As much as possible, everything we do to help employees learn should be experiential. We know that practice—spaced practice—is one of the best ways to ensure that learning is retained. Don't limit your thinking by calling the on-the-job learning effort "experiential."

Delivery Options

The practical aspect of on-the-job learning may make it one of the most beneficial for employees because it enables them to discover, make decisions, and deal with challenges that ultimately upgrade their job skills. The talent development role in this area is unique because the focus is on the supervisors as you help them find ways to increase employees' responsibilities and to learn from their mistakes. You will also help supervisors learn how to prepare their employees before attending any kind of learning event, as well as how to support them when they return.

You can use structured on-the-job programs to ensure employees gain the same skills, but it's more likely that you'll use informal on-the-job programs to develop individuals who have different assignments at different times. An IDP enumerates what each employee needs to learn or experience, and talent development professionals help ensure that the IDP process is as effective as possible.

Talent development professionals may be asked to provide or recommend assessments such as a multirater (commonly called 360-degree feedback instruments), team building, communication styles, or conflict management skills. Assessments provide an opportunity for supervisors, coaches, and mentors to open discussions about personal goals and developmental activities to grow and learn. As a coach to the supervisors, you may be able to guide them to ensure that employees see the value in the results—seeing the feedback as a way to further develop their careers rather than as criticism.

Delivery Support

Delivery for on-the-job learning is often trial and error. But it doesn't have to be. Matching the most appropriate challenging experience to the developmental need of the employee is powerful. It is your chance to put learning where the work is. You can coach supervisors to ferret out opportunities to match the right employee who has a developmental need with the perfect developmental opportunity.

Is your organization creating a team to address a customer problem? Who in the department needs to learn more about teamwork or how the organization addresses customer needs? Or perhaps a supervisor is leaving for a weeklong vacation. Who in the department can use that chance to learn more about organizing work, being a leader, or making decisions? Does the organization have a formal mentoring program? Who in the department needs to learn more about the politics of the organization? Perhaps the department's internal customer is very upset about something that the department screwed up—badly! Who in the department needs a stretch assignment to practice restraint under fire, negotiation skills, and conflict resolution?

Give supervisors the tools and techniques they need to successfully pair employees with the right opportunities, including checklists, guidelines, models, job aids, communication skills, delegation skills, providing feedback, and of course coaching skills.

Ideally, learning activities will lead to creative developmental assignments that help learners combine new skills with current skills. For example, a job-shadowing assignment may pave the way for the manager to offer the learner a role on a cross-functional team. This may in turn introduce the employee to another part of the company or to a potential mentor. As a professional development leader, you can help supervisors see the value in these kinds of assignments so that they can help their employees look for other opportunities. Every time this happens, it helps them extend the impact of the learning activity.

It is also important to coach supervisors to have productive career development discussions with employees. Help them understand the value of developing employees constantly, not only during an annual performance review.

TOOLS

"The 4Cs for Developing Others" is a tool to equip supervisors to develop their employees. Use it to guide a discussion about an employee's career.

What's Your Role in Selecting Content for On-the-Job Learning?

You probably have less of a role in selecting content for on-the-job learning. You do, however, have an obligation to ensure that managers know what developmental opportunities are available and how they can use them to grow employees.

In 2016, the Center for Creative Leadership surveyed tens of thousands of leaders and asked what skills were critical for career success. The responses included being a quick study, managing change, learning agility, interpersonal relationships, and collaboration (Scisco, Biech, and Hallenbeck 2017). When supervisors search for

TOOLS
"The Stretch Zone" is a useful tool to help supervisors understand how to focus a stretch assignment.

content that will help their employees, you can confidently share those five as a start.

Your role in on-the-job learning is more supportive coach and less trainer. You will work with managers, encouraging them to identify rotational opportunities and stretch assignments for their employees. You will help them see the value in sharing their tasks with employees and selecting a variety of employees to fulfill their role when they are out of the office—not just the department star. You can also suggest that they seek community and volunteer options that will help employees grow outside the organization. Keep managers informed about improvement or cross-functional team projects in which employees could be involved.

TOOLS
You can share "ebb's Supervisor's Employee Development Ideas Checklist" with supervisors who need to learn what opportunities exist for developing their employees.

What's in Your Implementation Plan for the 70 Percent?

What are all the possible options you may have for learning on-the-job, commonly called the 70 percent? Your implementation plan will include a coaching plan for supervisors; a list of possible job aids for supervisors to be better employee developers; a list of developmental ideas supervisors could recommend to employees; a list of job aids to support employees on the job; a communication plan to keep managers and supervisors abreast of learning opportunities; and a list of community and nonprofit organizations in the area that supervisors could contact.

Learning at Kohler

Kohler Co. was founded in Sheboygan, Wisconsin, by John Michael Kohler in 1883. He was promoting an enamel-coated "horse trough/hog scalder," which "when furnished with four legs will serve as a bathtub." This was the beginning of the Kohler plumbing business. Famous throughout the world for its high-quality, innovative plumbing fixtures, Kohler is also a model learning organization.

Laura Kohler, senior vice president for human resources, says, "We believe we can do almost anything if we learn it." Kohler's Learning Academy courses are so popular that most have a waiting list. Kohler marries the tradition of education passed down through generations of the Kohler family with new strategies that reinforce the culture of learning.

The ATD research report *Building a Culture of Learning* found that the essential traits of a learning culture are "closely aligned business and learning strategies, organizational values that affirm learning's importance, and an atmosphere in which learning is so ingrained that it simply becomes 'a way of life'" (ATD 2016). Interestingly, while only 31 percent of respondents described their companies as having extensive learning cultures, companies with high-performance metrics, such as market share and profitability, were five times more likely to be strongly identified as having a learning culture.

Kohler epitomizes the processes that create a learning culture (ATD 2016):
- Executives are involved in learning decisions.
- Leadership promotes learning.
- The culture of learning is built into the hiring practice.
- Employees are motivated by individual learning and development plans.
- Employees are motivated by advancement opportunities made possible by learning.
- Coaching and mentoring are organized.
- Learning programs are used to reinforce the corporate culture.
- Employees are empowered to stretch and take risks to learn.
- An environment of trust encourages on-the-job learning.

Each of these can be built into your talent development program.

Exploring Possible Support Services

Think about all the services that are tied to your talent development role. You may be responsible for your organization's talent management survey or addressing the results of the organization's engagement survey. You may be asked to conduct employee surveys, including multirater assessments. You might be put in charge of recertification efforts or college degree programs. Will you be asked to build teams or onboard new employees? Will you have to provide services that support IDPs, coaching, establishing mentoring programs, selecting high-potential candidates for your leadership development efforts, performance consulting, leading change, instilling agility, increasing innovation, or a host of other services your organization needs? Talent development is not defined as training or even training and development.

Think about the services that your organization will most likely need in the next couple of years, and how you can roll them into your talent development program. How will you manage it? What kind of budget will you need? What skills will your staff require? And most important, what is the payoff to your organization?

Roll-Out Plans

Your implementation plan lists the items that you will complete for each area: formal learning, learning from others, and on-the-job learning. Use this content to create a roll-out map that shows how and when each developmental activity will be available and who will be involved. Your map may also show how the plans tie back to the organization's strategy. Begin to communicate as soon as it is practical to do so.

TOOLS

The "Roll-Out Map Template" is a good planning tool and can help you organize everything in one place. It is located at the end of this chapter.

Once you have a strategy, goals, action items, and a general idea of the program's features, you can begin to establish a communication plan. You will most likely add to it and change it as you continue with the implementation, but begin planning early. Get the word out and update the communication plan as the program unfolds.

As you develop the communication plan, identify people who will need to know and those who will want to know, the specific information you want to share, the methods you have available to deliver the information, who will deliver the messages, and the timeline. It's important to get employees involved in the plan early, because this will increase buy-in and collaboration.

In the next chapter, we'll examine evaluation; for now, be sure that you tie the success of the talent development program into the communication plan. What went well? What will you improve? How is the talent development program affecting employees and the organization? These are great opportunities to obtain quotes from participants and their managers.

PRO TIP

Ask your marketing colleagues for ideas. They are experts in creating communication campaigns, so tap into their knowledge.

Think about the talent development brand and the consistent look you want to have. This will make it easier for employees to immediately recognize when something arrives at their desk or in their inbox from the talent development function. Consider using colors, symbols, or themes to tie together emails, resources, tools, and messages. You will also want to ensure that the talent development brand complements the organization's logo, colors, and other brand elements.

You may wish to invite different groups to a 60-minute meeting to introduce them to the concept. If possible, have a senior leader at each session to introduce the program and the plan. This demonstrates their support for the talent development program.

TOOLS

The tool "Communication Plan Tips" can help you develop your internal communication plan. It is located at the end of this chapter.

Incorporate the Effort Into Current Organizational Practices

If you are truly starting the first talent development program in your organization, you may not have other legacy courses or directions. However, spend some time thinking about other organizational activities and departments that may be connected to the talent development program. Some of these might include:

- a succession-planning process
- a set of competencies around which you want to build your talent development program
- a union, with which you need to coordinate.

Here are some additional questions you should think about:

- Have your leaders been involved in any sort of development effort, assessments, or university courses?
- Do you have any apprenticeship programs? How will they be incorporated?
- How is talent development related to HR, talent management, employee services, orientation, or other departments?
- Do external consultants or contingency workers exist with whom you need to coordinate?

Of course, if your organization has initiated other formal or informal learning events, be sure to review them before moving forward. You will want to have a uniform, consistent, coordinated plan across the organization.

Post-Implementation Steps

As you recall, *implementation* means that you have made choices and know what content you will deliver to whom. There is a likelihood that those formal events still need to be planned, designed, and delivered. One of the most important things you can do is return to your evaluation plans: Who is responsible for what? What are you measuring? What data do your senior leaders want to see? How will you evaluate your efforts?

You've Launched

With execution under way, you'll have long to-do lists. No matter how busy you are, stay connected to the managers in the business units and the senior leaders. They are your stakeholders and your customers. Communicate regularly so that you can keep them informed of your progress and learn what they may need. Continue to build the relationships.

Questions to Explore

- What skills and knowledge did the needs assessment reveal to you?
- How will you ensure that you balance your time among the ways that learning occurs in your organization, remembering the 70-20-10 guidance?
- What is the biggest concern you have for rolling out your first formal training session?
- What unique ways will you support employees to ensure that they learn from others?
- How can you assist your organization to implement a social learning platform?
- How can you work with other departments, such as IT and legal, to create a social learning platform?
- What tools will you need to bring supervisors up to speed regarding their role to develop their employees?
- What just-in-time tools do you have available to you?
- What value does your plan offer your learners? Supervisors? Leaders?
- How have you captured the drivers that are making this talent development program a priority?
- How do you define what success looks like in five years?
- Who is your target audience, and how do you know what they need?
- Who are the learning champions in your organization who can help you get this effort off the ground successfully?
- How's your executive team buy-in?
- What support services is your talent development program likely to offer?
- How carefully have you thought through your rollout plans? What can you do that creates excitement about the talent development program?
- What current organizational practices will need consideration and a plan for alignment? Do you anticipate any problems?
- Measurement is next. Are you prepared?

Tools for Success

Alignment Questions to Ask While Designing Formal Learning

Managers often ask talent development leaders to design training. Prior to designing a formal learning event, you may need to interview department leaders to clarify the problem they are trying to solve. You may also consider this an opportunity to educate managers about the importance of linking formal learning events to organizational goals. These questions can get you started.

- What organizational requirement will be addressed with the requested training?
- How is this training aligned to the organization's vision, mission, and values?
- What organization or industry issues are driving the training request?
- Is training the solution? Is it the only solution?
- If you could have anything you want designed into this program, what would it be?
- How will you support this solution?
- How will participants' performance improve as a result of the training?
- Who are the suppliers and customers who will be affected by the training? How will they be affected?
- How will we know we are successful?
- What will change one year from now?
- How far into the future will this effort reach?
- What can the organization expect as a return on its investment?
- What is the value of the results?
- How will we measure the value?

Used with permission from Biech (2009a).

Fifteen Quick Ways to Continue to Learn From Others

Are you looking for ideas to spark excitement about how employees learn from others? These can get you started.

- Start a blog tag. Write a short content piece and then "tag" someone in the content to respond and add to the learning topic. Keep them short.
- Create accountability partners as "living job aids."
- Organize personal learning groups to share best practices.
- Create a round-robin needs assessment where all learners share what they need to learn.
- Introduce the idea of having a team of learning advisers, much like an organization's board of directors.
- Develop a list of questions learners can ask one another about topics that are important to the organization or their departments. The goal is to create a dialogue.
- Assign learning buddies following a formal learning event.
- Start a "my one big thing" group, where each person collects ideas about the one big thing they need to achieve or improve.
- Encourage employees to create their own career path and work with someone to achieve the plan.
- Implement peer coaching circles.
- Initiate a LinkedIn or Facebook group.
- Encourage employees to visit one another's workspace and learn about what they do.
- Encourage the use of posting videos about how to do something.
- Create opportunities for employees to Skype with those at other locations to share what they know and what they learned.
- Encourage learners to volunteer for community settings and share what they learned from the experience.

The Stretch Zone

This tool is useful to help supervisors understand how to focus a stretch assignment.

Stretch and rotation assignments should push employees to develop just beyond their comfort zone, but not further. There are three performance zones:

- **The comfort zone.** When we are fully performing our role, we experience "unconscious competence" and mastery. We are able to perform easily and without exerting great effort. We do not find our work overly challenging— we may be doing just enough to get by if we get too comfortable.
- **The learning or stretch zone.** Just outside the comfort zone, this is where we leverage what we know and do well, and are able to focus our energy on new skills, tasks, or requirements. We are in a state of "conscious competence," where we are building skills but still have to be conscious of how we are performing to avoid mistakes and missteps. Our new responsibilities are manageable.
- **The panic zone.** If we push employees too far and stretch them beyond their capacity, they may become anxious, confused, and discouraged by so many unknown or unpracticed variables. Here we operate in a state of "conscious incompetence" and even "unconscious incompetence," which feels uncomfortable and which we would like to avoid.

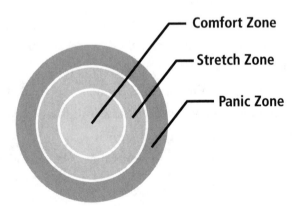

Yes, we could stretch someone too far. And we could stretch someone too little. The learner has to identify the sweet spot—the learning zone—to get it just right.

Used with permission from Azulay (2012).

The 4Cs for Developing Others

You may need to give supervisors the tools to develop their employees. Here's one to guide a discussion about an employee's career. The 4Cs encourage employees to consider whether various parts of the jobs they currently have are tasks they want to complete, continue, circumvent, or close down (stop doing).

As a supervisor, you need to plan discussions with all employees about their careers and future desires. You can initiate a career discussion using a couple of these questions that you think are appropriate to open the career discussion with each employee.

- What would you like your next position to be? How do you think you can best work toward reaching that position? What do you need to learn?
- What is your favorite part of your current role? What skill would you like to develop to improve your abilities?
- How is your present job preparing you for the goals you have set for yourself?
- What do you still need to learn about the position you would like to have?
- What would be helpful for your career development? What kind of training do you need to be more productive or successful? What experiences would be helpful?
- What goals have you set? Where do you see yourself in three years? Ten years?
- Who else can help you achieve your goals?
- What changes are needed to reach your goals? Can you achieve your goals in your present position?

Once you've started the career discussion, you will want to help employees consider the skills they need to accomplish their goals. The 4Cs tool can help identify these skills based on the tasks they currently do or want to do in the future. Begin by asking about the tasks they currently do:

- "What tasks do you want to be able to do that you don't do now?"
  - » List those in the position labeled *complete.*
- "What tasks do you enjoy and want to continue?"
  - » List those in the position labeled *continue.*
- "What tasks don't you do and would prefer to avoid doing?"
  - » List those in the position labeled *circumvent.*
- "What tasks do you currently complete that you want to stop doing?"
  - » List those in the position labeled *close down.*

Review the completed grid with the employee, asking questions such as:

- What does this summary tell you?
- What skills do you currently have that you could use to complete some of the tasks you desire?
- What skills will you need to develop to be qualified for the tasks you want to do in the future?
- What options exist that could allow you to quit doing some of the tasks you don't want to continue doing?
- How can I help you make this become a reality?

ebb's Supervisor's Employee Development Ideas Checklist

Share this checklist with supervisors who need to learn what opportunities exist for developing their employees.

Find Out Who They Are

❑ Meet each person at least once a month to talk about longer-term goals and new ideas they want to implement.

❑ Communicate with employees at least once a week to learn about their progress on their current projects, updates, and any struggles they are facing.

❑ Listen to them.

❑ Provide opportunities for 360-degree feedback options or other assessments.

❑ Identify specific books for each employee that help them understand their strengths and learning needs.

❑ Help them find a mentor.

❑ Hold them accountable for all they do.

❑ Introduce them to communication styles (for example, the DiSC or Myers Briggs Type Indicator).

❑ Provide performance metrics and create constructive conversation.

Help Them Explore Their Professional (and Personal) Opportunities

❑ Have all employees read leadership books and hold monthly discussions.

❑ Demonstrate how to seek feedback.

❑ Introduce employees to someone who can connect them to other experiences—such as someone in another department.

❑ Provide constructive feedback, always asking whether they liked or disliked certain tasks or parts of the job.

❑ Ensure that everyone has an IDP and uses it appropriately.

Show Them How to Learn

❑ Teach them how to network.

❑ Coach them.

❑ Allow them to struggle.

❑ Ensure that they have opportunities to experiment, fail, and learn.

❑ Create an ownership mentality by trusting them, providing experiences, and giving them authority.

❑ Share your own mistakes.

- ❏ Link them to a professional association or network.
- ❏ Provide a way all employees can share what they are learning.

Give Them New Experiences

- ❏ Turn over a small part of your supervisory responsibilities to them.
- ❏ Have them give a presentation to another department about what your department does.
- ❏ Invite them to conduct a lunch & learn about the department for the rest of the organization.
- ❏ Ask them to run a meeting in your absence.
- ❏ Find a project for them to lead.
- ❏ Take them to one of your meetings with the next level up.
- ❏ Offer development options beyond the job.
- ❏ Trade employees with other departments for a month.
- ❏ Trade employees with suppliers or customers of your organization for a short time period.

Explore Ideas for Development

- ❏ Use your meetings to share new skills or knowledge.
- ❏ Delegate something you like to do (not only what you don't like to do).
- ❏ Identify an employee for a stretch assignment instead of giving it to someone who can already do the job.
- ❏ Define the organizational politics and culture, and show them that politics isn't a bad word.
- ❏ Discuss how to navigate organizational politics.
- ❏ Lead them to classes, conferences, online learning, or other opportunities to develop them; spend the money to help them learn.
- ❏ Assign the work of an employee who is away learning to a co-worker. This gives the co-worker a developmental opportunity, and it also means the learner won't return to a stack of undone work.
- ❏ Help identify volunteer tasks outside your organization.
- ❏ Arrange for an employee to shadow someone in another department or a step or two up the chain.

Develop Yourself

Most important, develop yourself first. Be a model for life-long learning to build trust and to demonstrate credibility: accept feedback, be open to bad news and change, and invest in your own learning.

Roll-Out Map Template

Use a template similar to this one to organize a roll-out plan for your talent development program. You can also use it as a communication tool. You will probably start new pages for each learning type: formal learning, learning from others, and on-the-job learning. The map will show how and when each developmental activity will be available and who will be involved. Ideally, you will also include a column that states how the plan ties back to the organization's strategy. Example topics are included. Customize this tool to communicate the opportunities that are and will be available in your organization.

Learning Solutions: Putting Learning Where the Work Is

Formal Learning				
List Each Topic or Event	Delivery Method *(e.g., online, instructor-led, MOOC)*	Dates Offered	Targeted Audience	Strategic Alignment
External Programs *(e.g., university or certification courses)*	Registration Process	Current Dates	Eligibility	
Future Events *(e.g., guest speakers)*	How to Get Involved and Share Your Ideas	Quarterly Summary	Location	
Learning From Others				
Current Discussion Board Availability	Overview Information	Currently Ready	Current Learning Groups	Strategic Alignment
Match-Ups *(e.g., for accountability groups)*	Registration Process	Current Opportunities	Sign-Up Sheet Locations	
Social Network Availability	Future Plans	Go-Live Dates	Requirements	
Mentoring Program	Explanation and Preparation	Kickoff Date	Eligibility Described	
Future Planned Options *(e.g., mobile learning)*	Learning Solution	Quarterly Summary	Submit Your Ideas	

On-the-Job Learning				
Supervisory Coaching Available	Preparation Required	Date Selection	Additional Information	Strategic Alignment
IDP Support	Preparation	Scheduled Dates	Call-In Numbers	
Team Member Opportunities	Learning Solution	Current Availability	Current Listings Posted	
Job Aid Creation	Service Description	Service On Demand	Task Requirements	
Core Skills	Self-Directed	Available Now	Contact Number	
Planned Services				
List Future Services You'll Offer *(e.g., assessment options, team building, innovation lab, coaching, mentoring program, content curation, performance consulting, volunteering)*		Date When Each Service Will Begin	Comments *(e.g., who to contact, eligibility, description of service)*	

Used with permission from Elaine Biech.

Communication Plan Tips

Use these ideas as you develop your internal communication plan. You don't need a big budget; fun and creativity go a long way!

- Communicate often. Repetition is good. People forget and need to be reminded.
- Develop a notional timeline for getting the word out.
- Give the talent development program credibility by leveraging your leadership team—their participation will generate enthusiasm and demonstrate support. They should also be available to communicate informally.
- When possible, have your CEO announce key events.
- Use a variety of communication methods, such email blasts, messages from the CEO (that you write), flyers, newsletter articles, video teasers, podcasts, or posters.
- Develop tools that will be useful and practical to employees, such as FAQs, program overviews, and tip sheets.
- Make it fun with contests and branded items that you can give away.
- Create a list of events you want to share with employees, such as the first day of your first class, the implementation of the mentoring program, or the availability of a new social media tool.
- Keep it simple, using stories, metaphors, symbols, and analogies.
- Communicate to share program successes.

References and Additional Resources

ATD (Association for Talent Development). 2015. *Managing the Learning Landscape.* Alexandria, VA: ATD Press.

———. 2016a. *Building a Culture of Learning: The Foundation of a Successful Organization.* Alexandria, VA: ATD Press.

———. 2016b. *Kohler: Making Learning a Way of Life.* Alexandria, VA: ATD Press.

ASTD and i4cp (American Society for Training & Development and the Institute for Corporate Productivity). 2013. *Informal Learning: The Social Revolution.* Alexandria, VA: ASTD Press.

Azulay, H. 2012. *Employee Development on a Shoestring.* Alexandria, VA: ASTD Press.

Biech, E. 2009a. *10 Steps to Successful Training.* Alexandria, VA: ASTD Press.

———. 2009b. "Learning Eye to Eye: Aligning Training to Business Objectives." *T+D*, April.

———. 2015a. *New Supervisor Training.* Alexandria, VA: ATD Press.

———. 2015b. *Training and Development for Dummies.* Hoboken, NJ: John Wiley & Sons.

———. 2016. "The 90% Solution," *TD*, December.

Block, P. 2011. *Flawless Consulting: A Guide to Getting Your Expertise Used,* 3rd edition. San Francisco: Pfeiffer.

Driscoll, M., and A. van Barneveld. 2015. "Applying Learning Theory to Mobile Learning." *TD at Work.* Alexandria, VA: ATD Press.

Haddock-Millar, J., and D. Clutterbuck. 2016. "5 Critical Conversations to Talent Development." *TD at Work.* Alexandria, VA: ATD Press.

Reinhold, D., T. Patterson, and P. Hegel. 2015. *Make Learning Stick: Best Practices to Get the Most out of Leadership Development.* Greensboro, NC: Center for Creative Leadership.

Scisco, P., E. Biech, and G. Hallenbeck. 2017. *Compass: Your Guide for Leadership Development and Coaching.* Greensboro, NC: Center for Creative Leadership.

Tauber, T., and D. Johnson. 2014. "Meet the Modern Learner" Infographic. Bersin by Deloitte. www.bersin.com/Lib/Rs/ShowDocument.aspx?docid=18071.

5

Transferring Learning and Evaluating Results: How Do You Demonstrate Success?

In This Chapter

- How your organization determines success
- Available evaluation methods
- Impact on learners
- Impact on the organization

At first blush, it appears that this chapter is the place to read about evaluation and demonstrating success. That's only partially true. Think back to what you read in the first four chapters:

- Chapter 1: "Although we won't discuss the evaluation plan until chapter 5, you need to begin thinking about how you will measure success. What tools are available to you? What do you anticipate your leaders will want to measure?"

- Chapter 2: "This means that you need to begin the discussion about how you will evaluate the results. It is far easier to sustain a measured successful effort than one that is successful but has no data to support the success."

- Chapter 3: "End your strategy by identifying your indicators of success. How will you measure success and how will you demonstrate efficiency, effectiveness, quality, and the way the design meets the organization's needs? Present your evaluation plan: what and how you expect to evaluate the results."

- Chapter 4: "If you've followed the plan, by now you know what your leaders expect and how they will evaluate the program."

That's a pretty good argument for stating that you need to think about evaluation first, last, and all the times between.

Learning is a strategic enabler in your organization. That means that you and your talent development team are responsible for showing that talent development efforts are not only aligned to the organization's strategy, but actually produce a return on the investment. That return on investment could be substantial. Data compiled by the Korn Ferry Institute show that when companies align their talent strategy with their business strategy, the results may include:

- a boost in morale
- increased productivity
- lower turnover
- higher customer satisfaction
- better company financial performance.

You can demonstrate that talent development efforts contribute to these results with a good evaluation process.

With that in mind, what could I possibly add to what Don, Jim, and Wendy Kirkpatrick and Jack and Patti Phillips have already said in their many books? Of the organizations that have an evaluation process in place, almost all use a measurement method from one of them. Their techniques are well researched and proven. If you need an evaluation refresher, be sure to check out the books listed in the resources at the end of this chapter.

Determine and Demonstrate Success

No matter how perfect your talent development program is, most people agree that it is difficult to demonstrate a return on investment. So, what can you do to show business impact? Your measurement plan will begin with understanding what effect talent development will have on the organization. But it's not just the C-suite who wants proof. Think about who else needs to know. Then talk to your stakeholders about how you plan to measure success, and ask them for feedback on whether you're measuring the most meaningful items. In addition, consider your strategy for making recommended changes to any training or development events. Remember, you can't wait until the end to think about what and how you will measure.

Measuring the impact of implementing a talent development program may seem to be difficult—even impossible. However, if you identify your objectives—the reasons you are starting a talent development program—it is achievable. In addition to measuring performance, you'll want to monitor indicators that measure the development of the learning culture you are trying to create. For example, you could measure things like:

- how many employees have IDPs and what percentage of items were completed
- employee turnover or changes to engagement
- how many employees embrace self-directed learning
- sales growth in various regions
- decreases in accidents on the shop floor.

Depending upon the situation, some of these may simply be part of your strategy, such as increase sales or reduce accidents; but in other cases, they may be used as indicators of what you ultimately want to measure.

Early in this book you learned about the importance of communicating with senior leaders to identify organizational strategy, values, and goals. Those discussions become even more critical when we address evaluation because they provide the basis for what should be evaluated—establishing how the talent development program determines and demonstrates success.

PRO TIP

According to Wendy Kirkpatrick, leading indicators are short-term observations and measurements that suggest that critical behaviors are on track to create a positive impact on the ultimate desired results.

Talent development professionals need to show how the work they do contributes to organizational success. Multiple reasons exist for evaluation. A robust evaluation system provides valuable information for the organization, managers, talent development professionals, and of course the learner.

The organization benefits because the data show whether the learning strategy helped achieve the organization's goals. This benefit may be shown by return on investment or return on expectations. Evaluation can also provide a cost-benefit ratio and identify the bottom-line value of the learning strategy to the organization.

Managers benefit because evaluation can help them understand how to continue coaching their employees. It shows them the benefits of investing in staff, where the shortfalls may be, and what skills and knowledge have been gained that can be used as springboards to additional learning. Probably most important, the evaluation data demonstrate what has been transferred to the workplace.

Talent development professionals benefit because the data provide ways to improve the design of the learning experience. It can determine whether the objectives were met and to what extent. Facilitators can use evaluation data to determine whether the delivery and content were adequate and practical. Ultimately, evaluation helps to determine if any additions, changes, or deletions are required to improve the talent development program.

TOOLS

The worksheet "Questions That Turn Evaluation Into Action" at the back of this chapter lists questions you can use to begin determining how to utilize the evaluation process to benefit your organization, managers, and talent development professionals and their department.

Available Evaluation Methods

Many evaluation methods are available, so you will want to establish a framework for defining the value of learning for your organization. Many frameworks target the four levels of evaluation introduced by Don Kirkpatrick to guide their process of collecting, analyzing, and reporting quantitative and qualitative data on key performance measures.

TOOLS

Lisa Downs' "Comparisons of Learning Evaluation Methods" contrasts the evaluation methods most often used by talent development professionals from Brinkerhoff, Kirkpatrick, and Phillips. You'll find the chart at the end of this chapter.

As a reminder, the Kirkpatrick four levels are:

- Level 1, Reaction: Learner attitudes toward the training opportunity, such as a satisfaction with involvement or what was learned.
- Level 2, Learning: Knowledge and skills learned, such as being able to state the best practices or for having new skills for tasks on the job.
- Level 3, Behavior: Changes in execution and implementation of skills learned and practiced on the job.
- Level 4, Results: Quantifiable results that demonstrate the impact that training has on the organization.

We all know that most organizations are good at measuring Levels 1 and 2. Unfortunately, most talent development programs seem to shy away from measuring Level 4. However, you may be surprised to learn that Level 4 results are actually the simplest and least resource-intensive to evaluate!

According to the Kirkpatrick model, if something is a true Level 4 result, it is important enough that someone is probably already measuring it. That means it is simply a matter of obtaining the data. A true Level 4 evaluation measures a combination of the organization's purpose and mission, and it must be an organization-wide measure. The difficulty arises when trying to link specific learning events or training to the ultimate result (Kirkpatrick and Kirkpatrick 2015).

How to Get Started With Evaluation

You will be able to attribute your success to an excellent talent development program if you have a solid evaluation framework in place. The previous chapters mentioned the importance of having senior-level buy-in right from the start. They may not think about evaluating the talent development program immediately, but that doesn't mean that you can't open the discussion. As a conscientious employee, you have an obligation to do so.

Perhaps not immediately, but eventually, leadership will want a regular accounting that identifies the details and costs to develop employees, cost of various offerings, payroll, facilities, external suppliers, and so forth. To balance the cost, you will need evaluation to identify the benefits.

You have a chance to act as the conscience of the organization by ensuring that there is a maximum result for the investment in talent development. Senior leaders will increase their confidence in you and the talent development program when you commit to using metrics. You can get started by following a few guidelines:

- Start small. Don't think that you need to measure everything. Go back to your discussions with senior leaders and figure out what the program's purpose and strategic imperatives are. Then, identify a few leading indicators that you can use to measure. Start small and grow slowly to ensure that employees and processes are ready.
- Use the data. Once you have gathered the data, use it to drive the talent development program and business results. Success is dependent on demonstrating and quantifying the value in evaluation.
- Use qualitative data, too. The evaluations will also produce learner stories, examples, and feedback, which you can use to bring the data alive and to tell the talent development story.

- Use data positively. Ensure that everyone understands that evaluation is a positive part of the program. It should never be used in a punitive way. A proactive approach where you collaborate with leaders, supervisors, employees, mentors, trainers, external suppliers, and others demonstrates that you want to use the evaluation data to constantly improve the talent development program.

TOOLS

The "Sample Evaluation Plan" shows you one way to lay out an initial evaluation on a small scale. It is located at the end of this chapter.

Getting started with evaluation is a big task, so don't put it off too long! One of the easiest evaluation processes is a comparison. For example, think about how you can incorporate a pre- and post-evaluation strategy. The benefit is in interpreting results and showing the financial impact of the talent development program. It will help you to build a better business case for more learning.

TOOLS

"Data Collection Approaches" is a handout that presents the advantages and disadvantages of various ways to collect data. You will find it at the end of this chapter.

Cost-Benefit Analysis

Eventually you will want to present a cost-benefit analysis to your senior leaders. This tool was created in the 1840s by a French economist and engineer, Jules Dupuit. The tool affords you the ability to weigh the pros and cons or benefits and costs of your talent development program. The three steps are:

1. Identify the costs. This should include monetary costs such as payroll, equipment, suppliers, materials, participants' time away from the job, and so forth. It also includes nonmonetary costs, such as risks or productivity,

that could affect the organization. You will need to assign a monetary value to each nonmonetary cost.

2. Identify benefits. It may be difficult to determine exact amounts because other environmental actions may also have helped to create the benefit.

TOOLS
A simple "Cost-Benefit Analysis Template" is located at the end of this chapter.

Benefit values include profits, increased production, enhanced services, improved employee engagement, and others. You also assign a monetary value to each.

3. Compare cost to benefit. As you compare costs and benefits, consider how long it will take for the benefits to repay the costs.

Use your calculations to make recommendations for adding to, reducing, or changing the talent development program. The tool can also be used to make improvements or to rally for a larger budget. My best advice? Don't exaggerate.

Impact of Talent Development

When implemented thoughtfully, there is little doubt that talent development programs will benefit employees and the organization. Demonstrating impact isn't easy, but it is important. It is difficult to segregate what occurred due to the talent development program from other effects, such as changes in the economy, changed regulations, or new competition. But this should not stop you from establishing measures that demonstrate the impact of talent development on employees and the organization.

Impact on Employees

We know that employees change jobs more frequently now than ever before and that the reasons are often lack of development and a poor supervisor. An effective talent development program can address that for sure. But what else? Additional benefits that you might not expect can result from a good talent development program. These unexpected, yet beneficial spinoffs indicate that employees are not only more satisfied with their jobs and the organization, but more motivated and committed. Gaining new skills and knowledge increases their self-esteem and morale. If they are more informed and feel like they are part of the organization, they'll have more confidence in the organization's future. This also leads them to see more options for growth and development within the organization.

A talent development program can have a positive effect. Employee satisfaction and engagement are important to both the employee and the organization.

Impact on the Organization

When organizations support the talent development department, all employees and all departments can do their part to help the organization reach its business goals and objectives. Like any other aspect of business—research, marketing, sales, manufacturing—talent development requires an investment. Organizations also expect a return on their investment. In this case, that return will be expected in terms of improved customer satisfaction, higher sales, improved productivity, an overall increase in the bottom line, or better regulation compliance.

To increase the positive impact on the organization, you'll need to look beyond competence, look beyond training, and, instead, look at the entire system.

Competence, Commitment, Confidence

As talent development professionals, we tend to focus on skills and knowledge. While they are important, to have real impact for our organization, we need to go beyond them. Learners must leave every development opportunity with three accomplishments. We need to use the 3Cs—competence, commitment, and confidence—when evaluating learning and development opportunities to ensure we are delivering what our learners require.

The first one is easy and logical. We are supposed to improve our learners' knowledge and skills. That's competence. But if we do not also increase learners' commitment to change and their confidence that they can change, they will not implement the new skills, performance will not change, and everything will remain the same. Developmental events must help participants return to the job site and put into practice the skills and knowledge that were delivered. When evaluating learning opportunities, ask:

- Is content delivered that ensures learners' competence?
- Do learners have the commitment to implement what they learned?
- Do learners have confidence to be successful?

Is Training the Answer?

A lack of competence may not be the only reason performance is suffering. You also have to keep the six areas of human performance improvement (HPI) in mind. As a reminder, the areas that you can analyze include:

- **Physical resources:** The tools, technology, materials, and equipment performers need to do the job.
- **Structure or process:** The methods and steps that describe how work gets done in an organization, including the reporting relationships, incentives, and consequences.
- **Information:** How data are exchanged between people and machines to ensure information is consistent, accessible, timely, and in a useful format for performers—especially when used to make decisions.
- **Knowledge or skill:** Well-defined skills that are learned and practiced to perform a job; performers know how and when to use the skills.
- **Motivation:** Proper incentives to support the desired performance; the performer's values aligned with the tasks.
- **Ability or wellness:** Ensuring the performer is free of emotional and physical problems.

Each area can have limitations, be absent, or be misused, which will ultimately affect employee performance—even with the required skills and knowledge present.

Look at the Entire System

We also need to look beyond talent development essentials and HPI. Organizations are systems—the individuals and the processes within the organization are dependent upon one another. Talent development—improving individuals' capabilities and ensuring they have the right attitude—is important, of course. But as you continue to add elements to the talent development program, remember all the other factors that contribute to an employee's ability to contribute to and affect the organization's success.

From an evaluative perspective, begin to think more about what the organization needs in addition to what the individual needs to learn. What learning activities will build organizational capabilities, not just individual capability? How can coaching and mentoring broaden employees' focus and help them consider how to develop to integrate with other functions in the organization? Is there a way to assess the performance of the team, not just individual contributors? When identifying high-potential talent, is it possible to assign them to the teams that are more critical to contribute to the organization? These ideas may seem far-fetched right now, but treating talent development from a systems perspective is not.

The story in the sidebar about Credicorp in Peru describes how the employee development and organizational systems came together to make a major improvement.

Building Success at Credicorp

When Credicorp, the leading banking institution in Peru, set its sights on becoming a leading financial group across Latin America, a key to success was a leadership development initiative just as ambitious and robust as its business strategy. The goal was to create a leadership solution that would evolve in unison with the changing nature of the strategic challenges faced by the organization's leaders.

The Center for Creative Leadership began working with Credicorp on an initial leadership development program for senior managers in 2009. Seeing an opportunity to create strong links between their business strategy and leadership needs, the two organizations constructed a comprehensive leadership development architecture, including strong supports for learning transfer. Their developmental approach—focused on individual competency and collective capability—became the foundation of a broad and deep leadership strategy.

Every person in the leadership pool of 500 people worked with an executive coach to tailor an individual development plan aimed at strengthening the competencies most important for their success at Credicorp. In addition, each leader joined a learning and developmental support network in which they could share their developmental challenges and action plans. These accountability partners challenged and supported one another.

The concept of leadership development at the company shifted from delivering stand-alone training programs to ongoing learning experiences that stretch over a year and consist of face-to-face training modules, executive coaching, follow-on practice sessions, applied research activities, and strategic thought sessions with the senior leadership team.

With the new strategy and new approach to leadership development in place, Credicorp Group's revenue has grown exponentially, and the strategic plan calls for even more aggressive growth and international expansion over upcoming years. In March 2013, Credicorp was named by Euromoney magazine as the #1 Best Managed Company in the Banking and Finance Sector in Latin America, the #1 Best for Shareholder Value in Latin America, and the #1 Best Managed Company in Peru.

According to the *Wall Street Journal*'s MarketWatch, a large part of Credicorp's success can be found in the organizational commitment to high-caliber talent, the quality of its senior management, its ongoing commitment to corporate governance and sustainability, and the professional quality of its employees.

Used with permission from Reinhold, Patterson, and Hegel (2015).

Measuring Informal Learning

Having a learning culture is where it all starts. When employees recognize that they are responsible for their own development, they take learning more seriously and they are more likely to transfer what they've learned. When they learn the skills on the job, the results increase even more because there is no transfer, such as from a class. They needed help and they received the knowledge or skills immediately.

If transfer of learning is critical and informal learning is the way that most employees learn, can you evaluate informal learning? As a matter of fact, you can.

Informal learning activities, either learning from others or on the job, can be measured using tools similar to what you would use when measuring formal learning, such as questionnaires, appraisals, and opinion surveys. Platform-based social learning could be evaluated using the platform's analytical capabilities. If coaching sessions are included as part of the program, coaches might lead participants through self-reflection exercises to determine what they've learned and how they are using their new skills and knowledge. You might also be able to track learners' progress as they move around an organization. What do the patterns in the succession pipeline tell you?

Because evaluating informal learning usually requires different questions than formal learning, you'll need to modify Kirkpatrick's four-level framework. Here are some questions that provide a way to collect the data:

- What did employees learn informally?
- How did employees learn the informal content?
- How can employees receive recognition for their informal learning?
- What is the extent of participation in various informal learning activities?
- What is the extent of satisfaction with the resources used for informal learning?
- In what way does the organization benefit from the informal learning?
- Which informal learning efforts provide tangible benefits to the organization?
- How can the organization better support informal learning efforts?

(Carliner 2012)

TOOLS

Measuring informal learning does not use traditional methods. To capture data, use a format such as the "Informal Evaluation Worksheet" located at the end of this chapter.

Best Practices

Your organization is coping with dizzying rates of change, shifting markets, unexpected competition, a young and inexperienced workforce, and probably a shortage of leaders. A talent development program can and does resolve many of these concerns. However, to be effective, it must be targeted and aligned with the organization's strategy, and driven by the organization's business requirements. Keeping that in mind is the "best practice" you can achieve.

That being said, there are a few other best practices you can keep in mind when evaluating your talent development program. Let's look at some of them:

- **Have a plan and work the plan.** What you decide to evaluate in the beginning will not always work. Make sure you re-evaluate the plan at your annual review meeting. This is a learning experience for you, too.
- **Keep evaluations short.** When possible, make evaluations a part of the task if you want more input. If you ask for everything from learners, you will get nothing. Keep it short and easy.
- **Think long term.** Changes may not occur overnight, so be patient— learning is a long-term investment! While the benefits are not immediately obvious, they will be observable as employees become more knowledgeable and stick around. Commitment will build the organization's reputation as an employer of choice.
- **Focus your resources.** Resist the temptation to measure everything, everywhere. Too many directions can be overwhelming. Although evaluation is important, it is not the only thing you need to do.
- **Look for value everywhere.** Talent development can be costly. However, its effect can't always be translated into bottom-line dollars and cents. The result may be fewer customer complaints or an increase in sales. In these cases, tout good news stories or happy employees. After all, there are data that show the value in increased engagement.
- **Look for small things.** Evaluating boulders can be exciting, but it can also be risky. Focusing on pebbles will eventually add up to the kind of results you want to see.
- **Evaluation is good.** Do not use evaluation sheets as punishment—use them as a chance to improve. An employee who fails a test needs development. A facilitator who gets a poor evaluation needs development. A talent development program that is not living up to leadership's expectations needs development.

Evaluation Now and What's Next?

Evaluation gives you some insight into how effective talent development is today. The real value, however, is to use what you learn through evaluation today to create tomorrow. The data from evaluations—both quantitative and qualitative—provide a wealth of ideas for what you need to do next.

Questions to Explore

- How do you plan to transfer what you learned from senior leaders during your early interviews and meetings to the evaluation plan?
- What evaluation philosophy do you adhere to?
- What evaluation methodology might you experiment with?
- What specifically will demonstrate success the most?
- At this point, what do you think should be measured at the Level 4 category?
- What are the primary benefits of evaluation to employees? To managers? To the organization? To the talent development program?
- Several suggestions were given about how to get started with evaluation. Which one is most important to your organization?
- What would be included in your first cost-benefit analysis? Why?
- What are your thoughts about evaluating informal learning?
- How do you plan to approach the 3C conundrum: competence, commitment, and confidence?
- Looking at the entire organizational system as opposed to looking at improving individual competencies requires a holistic perspective. What are your thoughts, and how do you think they would align with your organization?
- What best practices would you add to the list?

Tools for Support

Questions That Turn Evaluation Into Action

This worksheet will help you determine how to make your evaluation more beneficial for your organization, managers, and talent development professionals and their department.

Organization

❑ What organizational strategies need talent development's support? How can we measure improvement?

❑ What business functions have the most impact on the organization's success? What can we measure to demonstrate impact?

❑ What roles are the most important to achieve the organization's strategy? What measurements would demonstrate this?

❑ What general capabilities do all employees need to support the organization's mission, vision, and values? How can we measure this?

Managers

❑ What core competencies are most critical to the organization's success? How can we measure improvement?

❑ What competencies will employees need in the future to address key strategies and business goals? What should we measure?

❑ How can the talent development department help you be more successful as you develop your employees? What should be measured?

Talent Development Department and Professionals

❑ What needs to be measured to ensure our skills are enhanced?

❑ What does the talent development department need to do better? How can we measure improvement?

❑ How are the talent development department's measures of success aligned with the organization's measures of success? What could be improved?

Used with permission from ebb associates inc © 2017.

Comparisons of Learning Evaluation Methods

This summary helps you see the differences between frequently used evaluation tools. Select an approach that will fit best with your program.

Kirkpatrick's Four Levels	Kirkpatrick's Return on Expectations (ROE)	Phillips' Return on Investment (ROI)	Brinkerhoff's Success Case Method
Level 1—Reaction **Level 2**—Learning **Level 3**—Behavior **Level 4**—Results (Impact) **Reaction:** typically measured through course evaluations **Learning:** typically measured through tests and knowledge checks during or after training **Behavior:** typically measured through surveys or interviews at certain intervals post- training to gauge behavior change and application of learning on the job **Results (impact):** typically measured through analyzing training's impact on business metrics, such as productivity, quality, revenue, sales, and decreased costs	Measurement is a partnership with the business; sometimes described as "the Four Levels in reverse" **Six Steps/Principles:** **1. Mission:** Identify the organization's highest-level goal and align program with this goal. **2. Leading indicators:** Identify these so they can point to a tracking system for results. Examples include employee retention, customer satisfaction, and new customer acquisition. **3. Critical behaviors:** Define what these are from the leading indicators. **4. Drivers:** Identify the processes and systems that reinforce, monitor, encourage, and reward performance of critical behaviors. **5. Design the learning.** **6. Monitor and adjust**	Often erroneously referred to as Level 5 of evaluation. Mathematical formula used to determine a cost-benefit ratio. ROI% = Benefits – Costs x 100 Costs A result greater than 100 percent means the program has a net benefit after accounting for the costs of running it. For example, an ROI of 200 percent means the program yielded $2 for every dollar of cost. A 100 percent ROI is typically the minimum for a program to continue. It's usually best to do an ROI analysis on larger initiatives and not on individual courses, due to the level of work involved in collecting the data, especially for monetary benefits isolated to the program.	Focuses on answering **two questions:** 1. What groups or individuals have been successful in applying a learning opportunity to achieve a business result and why? 2. What groups or individuals have been unsuccessful and why? **Five Steps:** **1. Impact mapping:** Identify the goal of the learning opportunity and determine how it's connected to business needs; this defines what success looks like. **2. Survey:** Ask participants for best and worst cases, such as how they've successfully or unsuccessfully applied what they learned to achieve a business result. **3. Obtain evidence:** Gather data that corroborate the cases. **4. Analyze the data.** **5. Communicate the findings.**

Used with permission from Downs (2015).

Evaluation Considerations for Formal Learning Events

Results are best when managers and supervisors are involved and aware of what formal learning events should produce. Use these questions as you consider how involved managers and supervisors are. Hopefully the discussion leads to additional valuable and informed conversations.

During the Formal Learning Event

- Did the pre-work and conversations ensure that participants were prepared as well as they needed to be?
- Did participants know why they were attending the training session?
- How well were participants able to connect what they do to appropriate business goals?
- Did participants know how they contribute to achieving organizational results?
- Are participants confused by mixed messages?

After the Formal Learning Event

- Are managers and supervisors involved in the follow-up as planned?
- Do participants know where they can receive support?
- Was coaching available as necessary?
- Are participants held accountable?
- Are managers and supervisors held accountable?
- How accurate was the measure of value?

Used with permission from Biech (2009).

Sample Evaluation Plan

Use this as a sample data collection design plan to present each program's objectives, how they will be measured, where the data are found, when measurement will occur, and who is responsible.

Level	Program Objectives	Measures	Data Source	When to Collect Data	Who
1. Reaction	Positive reaction, content, and administration	4.0 on a Likert 1-5 scale	Employee survey	End of classes	Program manager
2. Learning	Maintain 3.0 GPA	3.0 GPA out of 4.0	Employee testing	End of classes	Program manager
	Discuss purpose and employee role	4.0 on a Likert 1-5 scale	Survey		
3. Behavior and Application	Uses skills on the job	4.0 on a Likert 1-5 scale	Employee survey	Annually	Program manager
	Applies knowledge to other projects	IDP completion and performance record	Manager interview	One year follow-up	
4. Business Impact	Executive retention	Percent retained	HR	Six months	Program manager
	Promotable employees	Candidates ready	Succession review	Six months	
	Improve strategic results	On-time completion	Senior leaders	End of year	
	Recruiting success	Qualified candidates	HR	Monthly	
ROI	25 percent return on investment	Program manager calculates			

These questions will help you focus on what is important to include in your plan:

- What is your organization's philosophy about evaluation and measurement regarding employee development?
- What are the goals of the program?
- What expectations or leading indicators did you identify?
- What questions can you ask to clarify what your organization's leaders want to accomplish?

Data Collection Approaches

The tool you select to collect data should reflect the way the data will be used, budget, people available, and how much data you anticipate collecting. Be sure to pilot test your chosen collection tool. Here are a few advantages and disadvantages of each, as well as things you need to think about.

Approach	Advantage	Disadvantage	Think About
Interviews	• Can probe for clarification • Can be confidential • Good for rich qualitative data	• Time-consuming • More expensive • Requires skilled interviewer • Not anonymous	• Telephone or only in person • Use same questions • Allow for added comments
Focus Groups	• More efficient than individual interviews • Good for rich qualitative data • Can probe for clarity • Individuals expand on others' ideas	• Can still be time-consuming • Need skilled facilitator and notetaker • Not confidential or anonymous	• Group size • Method to record • Where to conduct
Questionnaires	• Easy to track • Easy to conduct • Can be confidential	• Usually a low-response rate • Can't follow up • Questions can be misinterpreted	• Online or paper • Length
Observations	• Data can come from a natural setting • Opportunity to gather and observe examples	• Requires skilled observer • Disruptive to work environment • Can be time intensive	• Skilled observer • How disruptive • Recording plan • On-site or simulated
Performance Data Reviews	• Can simplify collection • Can be lower cost • Less work for participants	• Data may not measure what is needed • Time-consuming if not in the right format	• Access to the data • Correct data that are required • Format of data
Knowledge Tests	• Easy to score • Captive audience • Can provide exact closure to objectives	• Only measures knowledge, not application • Some may not test well	• Timing • How to word questions • How to test for application

Cost-Benefit Analysis Template

Use this tool to help you make a case for change or improvement of your talent development program, or just one aspect of it.

Cost-Benefit Analysis Template						
Costs	Year 1	Year 2	Year 3	Year 4	Year 5	Total
Equipment						
Payroll						
Time away from work						
Travel						
Total Costs						
Benefits	Year 1	Year 2	Year 3	Year 4	Year 5	Total
Revenue						
Decreased costs						
Cost avoidance						
Total Benefits						
Quantitative Analysis						
Net Benefit or Cost	$	$	$	$	$	$

Informal Evaluation Worksheet

Measuring learning informally does not use traditional methods. To capture data, use a method such as those suggested by Saul Carliner.

What You Want to Evaluate	Methods Available to Evaluate It	Which Methods Suit Your Evaluation Needs and Why?
Informal learning at the individual level		
Identify what workers learned	• Self-assessments • Process portfolios • Coaching interviews	
Identify how workers learned it	• Process portfolios • Coaching	
Recognize acquired competencies	• Employee education records • Skills assessments • Certifications • Badges	
Informal learning across groups of workers		
Determine the extent to which individual resources for informal learning were used	• Analytics • Compiling data from evaluations of individual learning efforts	
Assess satisfaction with individual resources	• Surveys • Focus groups	
Identify the impact of individual resources	• Rater systems • Specialized reports • Long-term studies	

Used with permission from Carliner (2012).

References and Additional Resources

Anand, P. 2017. "Executive Dashboards to Win Over the C-Suite." *TD at Work.* Alexandria, VA: ATD Press.

Biech, E. 2009. *10 Steps to Successful Training.* Alexandria, VA: ASTD Press

Brinkerhoff, R. 2014. "The Growing Importance of Measuring Results and Impact." Luminary Perspective From Section V in *ASTD Handbook: The Definitive Reference for Training & Development, 2nd edition,* edited by E. Biech. Alexandria, VA: ASTD Press.

Bucy, M., T. Fagan, B. Maraite, and C. Piaia. 2017. "Keeping Transformations on Target." *Our Insights,* March. McKinsey & Company.

Carliner, S. 2012. *Informal Learning Basics.* Alexandria, VA: ASTD Press.

Downs, L. 2015. "Managing Learning Programs Step by Step." *TD at Work.* Alexandria, VA: ATD Press.

Kirkpatrick, J., and W. Kirkpatrick. 2015. "The Four Levels of Evaluation—an Update." *TD at Work.* Alexandria, VA: ATD Press.

———. 2016. *Kirkpatrick's Four Levels of Training Evaluation.* Alexandria, VA: ATD Press.

Levenson, A. 2016. "Measuring and Maximizing the Impact of Talent Development." *TD at Work.* Alexandria, VA: ATD Press.

Orr, J.E., I. Gochman, and M. McGowan. 2014. "Talent Strategy That Drives Business Strategy." Los Angeles: Korn Ferry Institute.

Patterson, T., S. Stawiski, K. Hannum, H. Champion, and H. Downs. 2017. *Evaluating the Impact of Leadership Development,* 2nd edition. Greensboro, NC: Center for Creative Leadership.

Phillips, P., and J. Phillips. 2016. Real World Training Evaluation: Navigating Common Constraints for Exceptional Results. Alexandria, VA: ATD Press.

———. 2017. *The Business Case for Learning.* Alexandria, VA: ATD Press; West Chester, PA: HRDQ Press.

Reinhold, D., T. Patterson, and P. Hegel. 2015. *Make Learning Stick: Best Practices to Get the Most Out of Leadership Development.* Center for Creative Leadership Whitepaper. Greensboro, NC.

Rothwell, W., A. Stopper, and A. Zaballero. 2015. "Measuring and Addressing Talent Gaps Globally." *TD at Work.* Alexandria, VA: ATD Press.

6

Planning Next Steps: Where Do You Go From Here?

In This Chapter

- What to do next if you are successful (or not)
- Ensuring that the talent development program continues
- Expanding to the next level: topics, tools, and methods to consider
- The organization of the future
- Your future in talent development

You may not have even started your talent development program yet, and here's a chapter about what to do next! Yes, you will be busy starting the program, but you will also have ideas about what you want to do next time, what you'd like to do better, or what you wish you had thought about earlier. Capture them. I like to carry note cards to jot down ideas for books that I intend to write. For projects like implementing a talent development program, I keep ideas in a folder on my phone or in a small notebook that I'll title something fun like "Genius Talent Development Program Ideas" or "Master Plan for Talent Development Program." I like using notebooks because I can take them into meetings with talent development advisory groups and quickly find data or ideas I want to share.

So, while it may be frustrating to continue thinking about what could have been, it is also the first step of ongoing planning, and where you go from here.

What to Do Next if You Are Successful (or Not)

No matter where you are in relation to the implementation phase, there will always be room for improvement. Take time to step back and view where you are today and where you want to be tomorrow. Focus your attention where it will have the most influence.

Most talent development efforts start out focusing on individual development that helps the organization achieve its strategic imperative. However, if you are also working toward making long-lasting gains in individual performance, and meaningful improvements in organizational learning, you probably still have a number of challenges.

In her book, *Learning for the Long Run*, Holly Burkett (2017) presents a model of sustainability for learning organizations that can be useful during the implementation of a talent development program. Very simplified, here are Holly's stages:

- Stage 1: Recognition, where the key question is, "How do we prove value?"
- Stage 2: Resistance, where the key question is, "How do we deliver value?"
- Stage 3: Renewal, where the key question is, "How do we add value?"
- Stage 4: Refinement, where the key question is, "How do we create value?"

RESOURCES

Learning for the Long Run, by Holly Burkett, is about establishing a learning organization, a topic we covered in previous chapters. Chapter 2 is the star of the book, introducing Holly's sustainability model.

This book presents questions that are similar to Holly's. The discussions you have with your leaders focus on proving and delivering value. When we came to evaluation in chapter 5, you were searching for how you added value. In that chapter (as well as some positioning and prodding in the first two chapters), I challenged you to lead the development efforts in your organization—not just as a talent development leader, but from an organizational perspective.

TOOLS

The "Sustainability Stages Checklist" can help you think about the actions *Learning for the Long Run* suggests you take to help you move through each stage.

Peter Drucker said, "Unless commitment is made, there are only promises and hopes; but no plans." So whether your talent development is wildly successful the first time or it is a dismal failure, you still need to take stock of where you are and make a commitment to take action to get to where you want to be next.

Ensuring the Talent Development Program Continues

You may be wondering what it takes to make your talent development program sustainable. Organizations are dynamic entities; therefore, an annual review process helps ensure the program grows and changes with the organization to meet its needs. The results of the evaluation process keep you focused on the right development efforts and tell the bottom-line story about the value of the initiative. Even if the evaluations show positive results, the talent development program will still require maintenance. And even if you are a one-person department, there are still steps you can take to ensure that your talent development program continues to be successful.

Create a Governing Body

You can create a talent development board, talent development advisory council, or employee development committee to help you make decisions about content, learning experiences, evaluation, budget, and other topics. The board can be made up of senior-level employees from

TOOLS

A "Sample Talent Development Board Charter" is located at the end of this chapter.

other departments across the organization. You will do most of the work, but they can serve as a sounding board, marketing adviser, and a connection to the strategy. They can also recommend improvements to the talent development program, and keep the lines of communication open to the business departments.

TOOLS

The worksheet "Exploring a Talent Development Board" will help you consider the details for forming a governing body. It is located at the end of this chapter.

Keep Senior Leaders Involved

To sustain the program, it is essential to keep your senior leaders involved. It's been proven over and over again: for any organizational effort to be successful, leaders must be involved. The rest of the organization will be watching and will take their involvement as a stamp of approval. Send out an email written by the senior leadership team, have them introduce new elements of the program, and ask them to speak about the talent development program. Ask them to serve as mentors and coaches, support cross-department developmental activities, or lead the way for developing direct reports. They will be viewed as the models for the rest of the organization.

Schedule Annual Updates

You will most likely hold reviews throughout the year, but make sure to dedicate time to review the talent development program at least annually with your governing body and/or senior leaders to make decisions about the future. What would be on the agenda? Changes to strategies, evaluation results, changes to learning experiences, budget updates, new efforts and designs, operational discussions, goals, trends and opportunities in learning, or other aspects of talent development that are important to your organization. The annual update is a perfect time to review what you accomplished and recount your successes, as well as look ahead to making improvements and what to introduce next.

Continue a Constant Flow of Communications and Marketing

Until it can hold its own, find ways to keep the talent development program in front of all employees. The communication plan you developed in chapter 4 is a good place to start. Keep communications flowing and the program visible throughout the organization. Tap into your leadership to be a part of the communication efforts.

Develop Continued Accountability

TOOLS
A simplified "Communication Plan Template" is located at the end of this chapter.

Build the talent development program into other efforts, connect it to events, and ensure that the organization's strategic documents reflect the initiative and its importance to the organization. Do what you say you will do. Keep promises. Admit mistakes. Improve continuously. Listen to your customers. Budget wisely. Stay focused on what is best for the organization and employees.

Expanding to the Next Level: Topics, Tools, and Methods to Consider

As talent development professionals and learning leaders, we have an obligation to stay ahead of the ever-changing landscape we call work and learning. Each year Deloitte University Press conducts research around human capital trends and publishes a human capital trends report. The 2017 report opened by stating that it "reflects seismic changes in the world of business. This new era . . . has fundamentally transformed business, the broader economy, and society" (Schwartz et al. 2017).

RESOURCES
Download a copy of the 2017 *Deloitte Global Human Capital Trends* report at http://bit.ly/2jkso2H.

"Seismic." That's huge! Colossal! Titanic-like! Are you ready? Let's look at some of the near-term topics, tools, and methods that should be on your radar now, if not already in your working toolbox.

Topics and Content

So much to learn. So little time. Your needs assessment will tell you what content your organization needs now and in the future. However, you should also be aware of general changes in topics that researchers see on the horizon. I have the good fortune to work with the Center for Creative Leadership (CCL). And although its focus is on leadership, I have always found its research to be a few steps ahead of everyone else's. The research is worldwide, and the studies usually include in excess of 10,000 participants. I am pretty confident in the results.

A recent study by CCL asked about the skills most needed to ensure career success. The five top critical skills were being a quick study, managing change, learning agility, fostering interpersonal relationships, and collaborating (Scisco, Biech, Hallenbeck 2017).

Beyond skills that ensure career success, CCL found that the four core topics that are always critical are communication, critical thinking, influence, and self-awareness. The addition of any of these topics would most likely make a difference in any organization.

Based on other research, I'd rate learning agility and collaboration as key topics to consider in this decade. And you might consider a little stress management. We are overwhelmed by data and inundated by information. Check the sidebar for some recent data about two of your favorite sites.

Data Overload

If you are feeling overwhelmed by content, data overload may be part of the reason. Data are being created faster than we can curate or consume it! Consider these examples.

Wikipedia
- There are more than 35 million articles in 288 languages
- The site logs 200 clicks per second
- This totals more than half a billion clicks per month
- 12,000 pages are created daily

YouTube
- There are more than 1 billion users
- Hundreds of millions of hours are watched daily
- 300 hours of video is uploaded every minute
- Half of all YouTube videos are viewed on mobile devices

Email
- We spend 13 hours per week on email
- This adds up to more than three months per year

Tools and Methods

You already know that today's learners are overwhelmed, distracted, and impatient. Where and how they learn is critical, and they want to learn from everyone: peers, managers, and experts. The good news is that today's learners are accepting responsibility for their own progress. They want to learn on their own terms and in their preferred space.

Your typical learner may be sitting in an airport with time to spare. She has a few minutes and turns to her smartphone to learn the latest highlights of the new effort your organization just rolled out. Will she find it? It's important that you are tapping into the tools and methods that work in your organization.

Learners want content they can download on their mobile devices. It needs to be short, on-demand, and curated so they can find it. They prefer social interaction or content that is continuous and integrated with their work, so think about how you can put their learning where the work is. We discussed the importance of supervisors developing people. That's the first part. The second part is determining how you can help learners be self-sufficient with both physical and electronic tools. Encourage learners to learn from their peers, and allow them to make the decisions about the best time to learn something new and perhaps even how much of it. Jane Hart writes about establishing a learning concierge service, for example, that would be like a "learning help desk" to provide personal advice to individuals on how they can address their own development needs (Hart 2015).

Given what we know about learners, what tools and methods might you review and consider for your talent development program in year two? Jane Hart develops a list of the top 100 tools for workplace learning every year. It is worth your time to look at her list to determine if some of the tools might be helpful to your talent development program. In the meantime, review the ones that are listed in the next few pages.

RESOURCES

Download a copy of Jane Hart's Top 100 Tools for Workplace Learning at http://c4lpt.co.uk/top100tools/top100-wpl.

Action Learning

"Action learning is a dynamic process for solving organizational problems, advancing individual skills, building teams, and developing leaders," says Bea Carson (2016), author of ATD's *TD at Work* issue on the subject. The elements of action learning include a team of four to eight individuals who are committed to learning, an action learning coach, a problem that needs a solution, and a process for resolving the problem that encourages questioning and good listening skills. Finally, the group is committed to taking action to resolve the problem. This is a good technique to consider if your organization needs to solve problems and benefits would be gained from working in cross-functional teams.

RESOURCES
"Breakthrough Solutions With Action Learning" is an ATD *TD at Work* issue that explains how you can use action learning.

Microlearning

This learning solution accommodates today's learners who want information in bite-sized pieces, fast and on demand, and specific to their needs. You should use microlearning if the skills or knowledge require repetition, can be chunked into small tasks, work in a digital format, and are practical and actionable. Your learners need to be motivated to learn, and you need to be able to support digital learning assets such as infographics, videos, or digital job aids. I contend that a job aid is the original microlearning tool.

TOOLS
"Sometimes All You Need Is a Job Aid" is a job aid to create a job aid. You'll find it at the end of this chapter.

Gamification

Gaming is an excellent learning tool, but one you may want to hold off on until your talent development program is more established. The high cost is usually the number one worry. Still most people rate serious games as being an effective tool for learning. Pay attention to how you will measure effectiveness.

PRO TIP

"Gamification is a bizarre word. What does it mean? Why does it matter? How can it be related to serious learning? These are questions I find myself discussing with my students and clients all the time. The only people I don't have to explain it to are my kids. They get it. They got it. They are part of it."

—Karl Kapp, *The Gamification of Learning and Instruction*

Blended Learning

Understanding the nuances of blended learning is critical. Blended learning is not like a cafeteria, where you take one of this and one of that. You will want to consider which learning technique is the best match for your circumstances and for the topic. I highly recommend another book in this series, by Jennifer Hofmann, who looks at blended learning solutions to determine how you can be effective and efficient, and save resources.

RESOURCES

Jennifer Hofmann's book in the What Works in Talent Development series, *Blended Learning*, will guide you through all that you need to know about the topic.

Learning Community of Practice

You won't want to wait too long before helping form a learning community in your organization. Learning communities (or communities of practice) help solve organizational problems and in many cases boost productivity. However, even more valuable is that they allow members to expand their professional knowledge. They can exist online or offline.

Here are several early steps you can take to start a learning community:

- **Establish the purpose.** Make sure you know what you are trying to accomplish before you put the word out. If you're starting a talent development program, it might be focused on how to ensure that everyone has access to what they need to develop.

- **Design carefully.** Put thought into the design. A charter is helpful because it lists the strategy, how communication will occur, what norms will be followed, who will be involved, who will serve as the moderator, and other important details. This ensures that everyone knows what is expected.
- **Allow input.** A learning community should be voluntary. Even though you want a clear plan or infrastructure to organize better, you still need to ask participants for input and be ready to change when a better idea arises.
- **Introduce everyone.** Plan a meeting where everyone can begin discussing their ideas and goals for the group. The initial meeting, whether online or in person, should allow plenty of time for everyone to get to know one another.
- **Schedule regular meetings.** Left on its own—especially during the initial stages—the learning community will be overcome by events. Scheduled meetings help members plan, and remind them of the effort. Monthly meetings help get the community of practice off the ground; switch to meeting once every two months to sustain the momentum as the group matures.
- **Plan for collaboration.** It should feel easy! Encourage an atmosphere of partnership and allow time for reflective discussions.
- **Communicate.** Use social media or online forums to communicate and provide a virtual home for your community. These platforms make working together easy, quick, and convenient. Publish a collaboration website to engage with learners.
- **Expect limited participation.** Don't be disappointed if you have only 10 percent participation. Like most organizations or groups to which you belong, most people watch and wait. It does not mean that they are not getting value; they are. Recognize the reality.

PRO TIP

Free is good! Use what you have. If you are worried that creating a learning community will be too difficult or too expensive, think of what you already have available. Many groups start with free tools, such as LinkedIn or Facebook, until they can create their own website. It doesn't have to be complicated or expensive.

Tapping into the collective knowledge and skills of the total workforce builds camaraderie and increases knowledge of employees. It also increases the sense of belonging to something worthwhile. Be sure to use the checklist at the end of this chapter as a reminder of key principles for designing a learning community.

TOOLS

The "Checklist of Design Principles for Learning Communities" can help you begin designing your learning community of practice. It offers 11 suggestions, along with questions to help you assess your effort.

The Organization of the Future

Dare we think about the organization of the future? Executives who responded to the *2017 Deloitte Global Human Capital Trends* report identified building the organization of the future as the most important challenge for 2017. Sixty percent of the respondents rated this issue as very important; almost 90 percent rated it as important or very important (Schwartz et al. 2017). This signals a shift, and agility plays a central role in making the change.

What does this shift mean? In the past, organizations were designed to be efficient and effective with predictable patterns. However, this design is not aptly suited to the unpredictability and disruptions facing organizations today—they need to be designed for speed, agility, and adaptability. This means shifting away from hierarchical teams to a more flexible model of small team networks. Innovation is the battle cry. Teams are formed and disbanded quickly depending upon the organization's need. And we know all organizations need to up their innovation game.

RESOURCES

The 10 Types of Innovation model will help you demystify innovation by offering a proven framework. A free app is available for you to download through the iTunes Store at http://apple.co/1IGSVsJ. The app also includes more than 100 innovation tactics.

What's your role in all this? As trusted adviser to your senior leadership team, you need to keep them informed of what's happening in other organizations. Help them embrace the speed of change by showing them the advantages of continuous feedback-based performance systems. Engage executives, managers, and employees as learning champions. Work with IT to integrate technology for more blended and social learning solutions. Make recommendations about the kind of development employees require so they can support future changes in your organization.

For example, as AI systems, robotics, and cognitive tools improve, almost every job is being reinvented, creating an "augmented workforce." This rapidly growing trend is causing organizations to reconsider job design and how work is organized. In the *Global Human Capital Trends* report, 41 percent of companies reported full implementation or significant progress toward adopting cognitive and AI technologies within their workforce. Another 34 percent said they are currently holding pilot programs. However, only 17 percent reported they were ready to manage and develop a workforce with people, robots, and AI working side by side (Schwartz et al. 2017). Is this a possibility? The January 2016 issue of *TD* published an infographic predicting that by 2018, 3 million workers around the world will be supervised by a nonhuman boss and 45 percent of the fastest-growing companies will have fewer employees than smart machines (ATD 2016). Do you have a clear role in this? Yes, you do. Figure out how you can lead this effort.

The Workplace Is Changing

Talent development programs need to consider the dramatic changes occurring in the workplace. Keep some of these commonly discussed changes in mind.

Freelance is here to stay.
Expect a 50 percent contingent workforce by 2020.

An organization's reputation is critical.
75 percent of job applicants will accept a lower salary to work for a reputable firm.

AI will rock the job market.
Expect 50 percent of all jobs to be completed by robots in the next decade.

Analytics will be key.
While 78 percent of companies claim they need analytics, more than 50 percent are not ready.

An information explosion is draining the workforce.
Organizations need to find a solution.

Imagine

Every industry and every job in the workforce will change. Here are a few examples. Imagine that:

- You require knee surgery. Your surgeon tells you he will not touch you during surgery, which will instead be completed by a robot using GPS coordinates.
- You have had a very long day and are now driving home. Your "attention-powered" car senses that you are sleepy and not paying attention. It takes over driving from you and slows down.
- You have a sick infant whose temperature requires constant monitoring. Your doctor applies a thermometer to his forehead that is no wider than a human hair.
- You've heard of 3-D printing, but 4-D printing is in the works too. And have you heard of bio printing? It's the ability to go inside your body and print new blood vessels or lung parts.
- Harvard researchers use a noninvasive brain technique so that one researcher's thoughts control the hands of another researcher.
- Imagine a fully interactive holographic room where you call up your learners around the world for a hands-on training session.

All of these not only are possible, but have been demonstrated today.

New Organizational Rules

What aspects of the organization of the future will affect you and talent development the most? Here's one big change. Currently, people become leaders based on promotion. It is likely that in the future they will become leaders by developing followers and growing in influence and authority. We see this today with what we call "informal" leaders. A second expected change is that advancement will occur based on many assignments, diverse experiences, and multifunctional leadership assignments. A third change is the elimination of fear of failure to grow, and instead fostering a culture of abundance and the importance of risk taking and innovation.

Think about those three changes. What does that mean for the plans you have for your talent development program? What will you need to change? How far away from the organization of the future is your organization?

The Future of Talent Development

Our organizations face an incredible number of pressures, and we must be prepared to lead the way to support them. Many of us consider ourselves trainers. The title *talent development professional* indicates the broader role for us, and it is required to lead the way. Where there are new challenges, there is a need for new knowledge and skills—for us and for our employees.

Our role has changed, and it did not wait for us to name or define it. Effective training and development may provide a solid foundation for helping our organizations overcome the challenges and pressures they face, but there is so much more. We are asked to take on more responsibilities and to find new ways to relieve the pressure our organizations face. We are a part of the fabric that makes up our organizations, and we touch everything, so it is no wonder our roles and responsibilities have expanded.

How many of these new roles do you anticipate building into your talent development program?

- Onboarding new employees?
- Leading change initiatives?
- Coaching managers to take on a developmental role?
- Establishing mentoring programs?
- Leading informal and social learning initiatives?
- Providing internal consulting?
- Conducting team building initiatives?
- Advising the C-suite?

You are expected to take on all tasks as a talent development professional and leader. Do you have the organizational awareness to do so?

RESOURCES

Learn more about how to increase your organizational understanding by reading the chapter "Building Your Business Acumen," by Kevin Cope, in the *ASTD Handbook: The Definitive Reference for Training & Development.* Cope provides seven steps for building business acumen: committing time, talking with key managers, being proactive, making outside contacts, finding a mentor, influencing management, and increasing your value.

Are You Meeting Expectations Today?

Think about the workplace of today and consider the employees entering the workforce. Do your talent development plans meet the requirements of your organization?

Do your plans meet the expectations of the learners who are entering the workforce in your organization? Review these expectations to decide whether your talent development plans are meeting these expectations.

- Learner expectations:
    - » Designing in microbursts?
    - » Simplifying work?
    - » Incorporating cognitive science?
    - » Using short, on-demand videos for learning?
    - » Implementing m-learning?
- Organizational expectations:
    - » Aligning a MOOC strategy to your organizational strategy?
    - » Curating content?
    - » Providing C-suite solutions?
    - » Accommodating the development and other needs of the nontraditional workforce?
    - » Redesigning the managers' and supervisors' skill sets?
    - » Tapping into the less expensive systems to capture, create, and publish content?
    - » Focusing on how we learn?

Are You Prepared to Address Learning of the Future?

Imagine a situation where:

- The classroom goes to the learner.
- We each have personally curated content in our hands.
- All learning is individually customized.
- Learning is lifelong focused and connected.
- Learning occurs in an augmented reality.
- Interaction occurs in holographic rooms.

Or maybe one day we'll be able to use *Star Trek*'s Holodeck and Transporter.

The future holds exciting opportunities for how employees will develop, as well as the skills they will need. I know what you're probably thinking: You are just starting a talent development program for your company, and I am already asking you to think about the changes! It's true. You are probably OK doing what you are doing now, but you may need to re-engineer your talent development function sooner than you think! Your organization needs you to be more innovative than ever to help it move into the future.

There are many new things you can or should do. You also need to be a good role model for all those around you. If you've been leading a talent development program for a while, you are probably doing many "things." The challenge is to identify which of those things you can stop doing. Stopping something you don't need is just as important as starting something new that you do need.

The End Is the Beginning

No matter where you are in the implementation of your talent development program, you are probably filled with ideas and eager to get started. You've reached the end of the book, but it is only the beginning of the exciting things you have ahead of you. And although this chapter addresses the importance of making improvements, it's also meant to prepare you for future planning.

Today you need to focus your attention where it will have the most impact for your learners and your organization. Use the questions here to think about the future, the skills you will need, where you will find experts who can mentor you, and what excites you the most about your organization's talent development future.

Questions to Explore

- How can you capture ideas about improvements that you want to make to the talent development program?
- How will you ensure that the talent development program is sustainable now and in the future?
- What will you do to ensure sustainment of the talent development program?
- If you plan to have a talent development advisory board, who should be on it? Why?
- How do you intend to keep your senior leaders involved?
- Which tool or method will you implement next? Why?
- Where can you gather preliminary data about the acceptance of new tools or programs in your organization?
- Starting a community of practice early can be beneficial. What are the advantages to your organization? What roadblocks might you hit?
- What excites you about the organization of the future?

- What frightens you about the organization of the future?
- What skills and knowledge do you need to develop, refine, or enhance to stay ahead of what is happening in your organization and your industry?
- How will you develop these skills? Who has the expertise? When will you set time aside to learn?
- How's your quitting quotient? That is, how easy is it for you to stop offering services or end a program to make room for new actions?

Tools for Support

Sustainability Stages Checklist

Use this checklist to consider essential actions you can take to move through each stage.

Key Actions for Each Stage	What Will You Do to Address This Stage?
Stage 1: Recognition, the key question is, "How do we prove value?"	
Align learning and business strategies	
Engage leadership support	
Link learning to performance	
Establish a measurement framework	
Stage 2: Resistance, the key question is, "How do we deliver value?"	
Educate and advocate	
Build capabilities	
Deploy well	
Develop partnerships	
Show how learning and performance solutions solve real problems	
Stage 3: Renewal, the key question is, "How do we add value?"	
Communicate relentlessly	
Stabilize infrastructure	
Strengthen alliances	
Measure what matters	
Incorporate continuous improvement mechanisms	
Stage 4: Refinement, the key question is, "How do we create value?"	
Foster change resilience and agility	
Embrace innovation mindsets and practices	
Continually reflect, review, and refine	

Adapted with permission from Burkett (2017).

Forming a Talent Development Board

If you are considering creating a governance body to help you make decisions or advise you about the talent development program, this worksheet can provide some guidance.

Feature	Options and Thoughts	Organizational Preference
Name	Talent development board, talent development advisory council, or employee development committee	
Purpose	Make decisions, provide input, make suggestions, give advice, or more of a working group	
Topics	Content, learning experiences, evaluation, budget	
Number of Members	Recommend 5 to 7; mostly depends on how many departments need representation	
Representation	High-profile departments, HR	
Meeting Frequency	Once a month for an hour	
Benefit	Go-to team when a decision needs to be made or issues arise	
Drawbacks	One more thing to do, too many ideas, time investment	
Leader	Talent development manager or circulating every 6 months	
Meeting Attendance	Send a substitute or not, mandatory attendance	
Membership Term	1 to 2 years	
Selection Process	Appointed, volunteer, recommendation by immediate supervisor or manager	
Selection Criteria	Level in the organization, leader, informal leader	
Employee Representation	Members beyond those who have supervisory responsibilities	
Other Locations	Foreign countries, other domestic locations	
Unique Needs	Shift employee representation, union representation	

Sample Talent Development Board Charter

A charter is a good way to ensure there are no questions about the purpose of the board. Use this sample to get you started.

Talent Management Board Charter

Background: The CEO's direction on January 25, 2017, provides for the development of an organizational human capital strategy and an implementation plan to include:

- An assessment of workforce requirements and characteristics for future needs
- Identification of human capital strategies with supporting goals, priorities, and performance measures aligned to the mission, goals, and objectives
- Processes to:
  - » Integrate human capital strategy into the budget and strategic plans.
  - » Address skills gaps, recruitment, development, sustainment, and succession planning for an agile, high-performing, innovative, and committed workforce.
  - » Ensure leadership accountability and continuous process improvement.

The organization's human capital strategic and implementation plans have begun. A major organizational change such as this requires a guiding coalition to:

- Anchor new approaches deep in the culture.
- Address questions and related issues.
- Eliminate key obstacles preventing the organization from moving forward.
- Keep the organization abreast of human capital efforts.

Purpose: The talent management board operates in an advisory capacity to the CEO and provides leadership accountability to processes that support the evolving human capital design. The board's work may include, but is not limited to:

- Monitor competencies relevant to the organization's future success.
- Review career development strategies, such as using 360-degree tools, developing an organization academy of learning, using IDPs, or improving new employee orientation.
- Review candidates for academic studies and fellowships, special management and executive development programs, and long-term development.

- Make recommendations for issues that affect the workforce, such as the best use of science fellows and interns, implementing regulations, or identifying future talent needs.
- Address organization-wide issues, such as diversity needs, succession planning, the mentoring process, and the competency management system.
- Align recruitment and retention strategies with workforce planning to enhance each strategy and close critical position and competency gaps.
- Make sure that the human capital strategy is aligned with the organization's strategy.
- Review and recommend annual human capital budgets.

The board shall utilize the combined acumen of interdepartment teams to identify, analyze, and resolve board issues.

Membership: Members include two S&T department heads (to be rotated biannually among all S&T departments), the vice president of business operations, the comptroller, and one ad hoc member recommended by the executive team. The director of talent management shall facilitate the meetings. The director of HR shall serve as the board's executive secretary.

Schedule and Deliverables: The board will meet monthly and deliver an annual *State of the Human Capital Strategy* report to the CEO.

Communication Plan Template

Use this basic tool to develop your communication plan.

Date	Targeted Audience	Message or Event	Method or Media	Who Delivers	Notes
May 13	Supervisors	Managers must develop employees	Email from CEO Lunch & Learn	CEO Finance VP	Talent development department develops material

Design Principles for Learning Communities

This tool outlines the key principles for designing a learning community. In addition, it includes a few questions to help you assess whether your strategies are supporting the principles.

1. Deliver measurable business results.
   - » What are the key business drivers?
   - » What is the desired impact on business goals and objectives?
   - » How will you gather data (qualitative and quantitative), analyze it, and report it?
   - » What organizational systems help sustain learning? What organizational systems are inconsistent with this?
   - » Is knowledge demand-driven and does it focus on value-added areas?

2. Integrate learning into day-to-day work.
   - » Where is the majority of learning time spent (in the classroom or on the job)?
   - » Have you provided tools and techniques that are practical and useful?
   - » Have you created a process to gather feedback and results?
   - » What processes are in place to support knowledge generation?
   - » Will the learning occur in a meaningful context, and is it integrated with actual work?

3. Support a long-term focus.
   - » Do you promote double- and multiloop learning?
   - » Have you provided enough information to all stakeholders to help them take the long-term view?
   - » Have you encouraged stakeholders to tolerate a certain amount of uncertainty and ambiguity?
   - » Does the learning program promote a sufficient level of exploration (rather than prescribe a certain approach)?
   - » Is your design flexible? Are there iterative steps for review? Is the process open ended (not event focused)?

4. Increase choices rather than pursue one (right) way.
   - » Do your programs expand thinking?
   - » Are members challenged to make choices to arrive at better decisions?

» Are you resisting prescriptions for success?

» Are you including thought leaders from a variety of areas?

» Does the learning encourage and accommodate a diversity of approaches and styles?

5. Allow feedback to drive enhancements.

» Is your design flexible enough to quickly allow for changes and improvements?

» Is the process becoming more efficient and effective every time?

» Can you quickly assess where improvements are needed (in both the product and the process)?

» Is everyone involved encouraged to provide feedback and suggestions?

» Do you acknowledge that hindsight is better than foresight?

6. Design programs so that they are easily maintained.

» Are you leveraging technology to facilitate learning and maintenance?

» Is energy fed into the program on a regular basis to provide growth and renewal?

» Is maintenance an ongoing and iterative part of the process (not an event)?

» Is technology used to share updates with everyone? Are new versions of the materials easily accessible?

7. Learn from the process, not just the product.

» Did everyone involved learn something from this experience?

» Did the learning extend beyond those directly involved?

» Can you gain insights from the way you learned, in addition to the content you learned?

» What tools for reflection have you used?

» Have you created a network of peers, facilitators, and mentors?

8. Include a variety of learning experiences.

» Are you allowing for a diversity of styles and preferences in terms of how people learn, think, and communicate?

» How will you achieve a balance of media, activities, and so forth to support the process?

9. Ensure learning is inclusive, not exclusive.

» Will this program serve all regions, services, and groups? If yes, are all regions, services, and groups included from the beginning?

» Is there a sense of shared success and shared risk among the various stakeholders and constituents?

» What vehicle or process is in place to ensure inclusion and promote collaboration?

» What work practices will sustain inclusion?

10. Promote mindful learning.

» What elements of the program support mindful learning?

» Will the learning occur in a context that is similar to the work context?

» Does the learning contain examples, cases, activities, and discussions that link directly to the work environment?

» How can learning opportunities be built into organization-wide practices?

» What occurs outside the classroom to ensure that the learning is context based?

11. Consider culture and values.

» Does the community promote healthy dialogue around the culture and values of individuals, teams, and the organization?

» Have you considered both implicit and explicit culture and values?

» Is there sufficient "tension" to indicate that you are continuously challenging learners?

» Are there opportunities to reflect on and re-evaluate your values in connection with your current and future challenges?

12. Seek ownership through partnership.

» Does everyone understand and accept the shared risks and shared successes?

» Do you constantly look for ways to build and rejuvenate a sense of ownership?

» Is there an acceptable level of trust and respect among all the people involved?

» Are issues and agreements made explicit?

» Do you have processes in place to freely share information and obtain input from everyone?

Used with permission from Voosen and Conneely (2002).

Sometimes All You Need Is a Job Aid

Use a job aid when the task is performed infrequently and self-correction is possible. A job aid can produce immediate and accurate performance, as well as predictable results. This list of job aids shows the wide variety available.

Type of Job Aid	Description	When It Might Be Used
Reminder	Prompt with simple instructions, such as actions for using a tool safely	Simplest version, used as a cue to do or not do something
Match	An example or model, such as a picture of how something should look	When a visual is available to demonstrate accuracy
Decision Tree	A list of factors to consider before making a decision, such as considerations for health eligibility	When many factors are based on criteria or issues; may have different starting points
Checklist	A list, sometimes in sequence, such as the list of supplies required for a workshop	Reminder of tasks to complete, but not necessarily in order
Template or Form	A preset format that limits how something is created	When standardization is important or to save time
Step-by-Step	Sequenced performance, such as how to set an alarm system or use ADDIE	When a series of steps are followed in order
Flowchart	Shows the sequence in diagram format, such as some instructional design processes or the HPI model	When a visual road map is useful or decisions must be made
Decision Table or Tree	Content that can be placed in rows and columns for quick reference	When an if-then format is required
Worksheet	Shows the final product as an example to model	When an example of a format or calculation is useful
Reference Source	Provides final decision authority, such as a dictionary	When a source is required to confirm or identify information
Script	Wording to follow for specific instances, such as handling an irate customer	For human interaction to lead to a positive result
Troubleshooting Diagram	Graphic that helps diagnose and select the right option	When multiple possibilities exist for complex problems
Mnemonic	Verbal, image, rhyme, or acronym to help remember, such as SMART objectives	Often used in conjunction with other job aids
Mistake Proofing or Poka Yoke	Japanese in origin, adopted by lean manufacturing, modifies equipment or tools to reduce or eliminate errors	When automation or color coding prevents mistakes before they occur

Adapted with permission from Willmore (2006).

References and Additional Resources

ATD (Association for Talent Development). 2016. "Technology: The Good, the Bad, and How We'll Work in the Future." Infographic. *TD*, January, 17.

Biech, E. 2015. *Training Is the Answer: Making Learning and Development Work in China.* Fairfax, VA: Trainers Publishing House.

Burkett, H. 2017. *Learning for the Long Run: 7 Practices for Sustaining a Resilient Learning Organization.* Alexandria, VA: ATD Press.

Carson, B. 2016. "Breakthrough Solutions with Action Learning." *TD at Work.* Alexandria, VA: ATD Press.

Cope, K. 2014. "Building Your Business Acumen." Chapter 43 in *ASTD Handbook: The Definitive Reference for Training and Development*, edited by E. Biech. Alexandria, VA: ASTD Press.

Hart, J. 2015. *Modern Workplace Learning: A Resource Book for L&D.* Centre for Learning and Performance Technologies.

Hofmann, J. 2018. *Blended Learning.* Alexandria, VA: ATD Press.

Johansen, B. 2012. *Leaders Make the Future: Ten New Leadership Skills for an Uncertain World,* 2nd ed. San Francisco: Berrett-Koehler.

Kapp, K. 2012. *The Gamification of Learning and Instruction.* San Francisco: John Wiley & Sons.

Margol, E. 2017. "Microlearning to Boost the Employee Experience." *TD at Work.* Alexandria, VA: ATD Press.

Pasmore, B., and S. Taylor. 2017. "Core Competencies Remain Critical to Success." *Workforce*, January 19. www.workforce.com/2017/01/19/core-competencies -remain-critical-success.

Petrie, N. 2014. *Future Trends in Leadership Development.* Greensboro, NC: Center for Creative Leadership.

Petrie, N. 2015. *The How-To of Vertical Leadership Development—Part 2.* Greensboro, NC: Center for Creative Leadership.

Ruderman, M.N., C. Clerkin, and C. Connolly. 2014. *Leadership Development Beyond Competencies: Moving to a Holistic Approach.* Center for Creative Leadership White-paper. www.ccl.org/articles/white-papers/leadership-development-beyond -competencies-moving-to-a-holistic-approach.

Schwartz, J., L. Collins, H. Stockton, D. Wagner, B. Walsh. 2017. *Rewriting the Rules for the Digital Age: 2017 Deloitte Global Human Capital Trends.* Westlake, TX: Deloitte University Press.

Scisco, P., E. Biech, and G. Hallenbeck. 2017. *Compass: Your Guide for Leadership Development and Coaching.* Greensboro, NC: Center for Creative Leadership.

Smith, A. 2016. "10 Tools for Organizational Development." *TD at Work.* Alexandria, VA: ATD Press.

Voosen, D., and P. Conneely. 2002. "Building Learning Communities." *Infoline.* Alexandria, VA: ASTD Press.

Willmore, J. 2006. *Job Aids Basics.* Alexandria, VA: ASTD Press.

Acknowledgments

Many wise and wonderful people worked behind the scenes to make this a comprehensive and practical book. Thank you to Amanda Smith—even though you jumped ship halfway through to deliver beautiful Cairo—and Justin Brusino, who always offers sound advice.

Thanks to everyone at ATD Press, who take care of all the difficult parts of producing a book, allowing me to do all the exciting parts: Kathryn Stafford, whose queries and questions ensured the book would be an easy read; Melissa Jones, who prodded my prepositions into place and kept the grammar gods contented. Thanks also goes out to Caroline Coppel, proofreader extraordinaire, and design artists Fran Fernandez and Iris Sanchez (with a little help from beautiful baby Ava).

Finally, thank you to my readers—especially those of you who tell me how you use the content in my books. It is rewarding to know my words work for you!

About the Author

Elaine Biech, president of ebb associates inc, a strategic implementation, leadership development, and experiential learning consulting firm, has been in the field for more than 30 years helping organizations work through large-scale change. She has presented at dozens of national and international conferences, and has been featured in publications such as the *Wall Street Journal, Harvard Management Update, Investor's Business Daily,* and *Fortune.* She is the author and editor of more than 75 books, and received national awards for two of them.

Among her extensive body of published work are many ATD titles, including the flagship publication, *The ASTD Handbook: The Definitive Reference for Training & Development* (2014). Other ATD titles include *The Art and Science of Training* (2017), *Change Management Training* (2016), *New Supervisor Training* (2015), *The Book of Road-Tested Activities* (co-published with Pfeiffer, 2011), *ASTD Leadership Handbook* (2010), *ASTD's Ultimate Train the Trainer* (2009), *10 Steps to Successful Training* (2009), *ASTD Handbook for Workplace Learning Professionals* (2008), and *Thriving Through Change: A Leader's Practical Guide to Change Mastery* (2007).

Elaine specializes in helping leaders maximize their effectiveness. Customizing her work for individual clients, she conducts strategic planning sessions and implements corporate-wide systems, such as quality improvement, change management, re-engineering of business processes, and mentoring programs. Elaine is a consummate training professional, facilitating training on a wide range of workplace and business topics. She is particularly adept at turning dysfunctional teams into productive ones. As a management consultant, trainer, and designer, she provides services globally to public- and private sector organizations to prepare them for current challenges.

A longtime volunteer for ATD, Elaine has served on the association's national board of directors, was the recipient of the 1992 ASTD Torch Award, the 2004 ASTD Volunteer Staff Partnership Award, and the 2006 Gordon Bliss Memorial Award. In

2012, she was the inaugural CPLP Fellow Program Honoree from the ATD Certification Institute. Elaine was instrumental in compiling and revising the CPLP study guides. She wrote the first ASTD Training Certificate Program and has designed five additional certificate programs. She was the 1995 Wisconsin Women Entrepreneur's Mentor Award recipient, and has served on the Independent Consultants Association's Advisory Committee, and the Instructional Systems Association board of directors. Elaine is currently a member of the Center for Creative Leadership's (CCL) board of governors and is the chair for CCL's Research, Evaluation, and Societal Advancement Committee.

Index